Rahul S. Verghese is a graduate of the Indian Institute of Management at Ahmedabad, India's premier business school. He worked for 25 years with Unilever, Nestlé, a garment company, and Motorola in varied national, regional, and global marketing as well as business management roles. He then switched gears to start a venture to build running into a marketing platform, to enable brands, organizations, and individuals to unleash their potential.

Rahul loves adventure. He started trekking and rock climbing while in school, mountaineering while attending St Stephen's College, river rafting in his late twenties, and skiing and running when he hit his 40s. He ran and walked on his newly-bought treadmill for six months during his first encounter with the cold Chicago winter, and exulted when he ran five kilometres without stopping. Two months later he signed up for the Chicago Marathon — and completed it. A year later he improved his time in the marathon — and got bitten by the running bug. He has now run over 51 marathons in 6 continents. A key goal of his business venture is to inspire 200 million people into enjoying running.

Rahul has shaken hands with world champion athletes, spoken to leading doctors, read several medical reports, run with thousands of amateur runners like himself in marathons across the world, chatting and clicking photographs along the way. Being an accidental runner, he has learnt a lot about the "how to" and now, increasingly, about the "why" of running from several people across the world who have run in the over 200 runs his company has organised across India, and from those who visit his company's website — www.runningandliving.com.

His company Running And Living Infotainment, is focused on being a 360 degree marketing platform (online/ offline/ relationship builds / social media and community connects) for companies and brands, and organizes 5-kilometre to ultra marathon runs in more than 10 states of India, helps social causes, holds informative sessions, and mobilizes networking opportunities at these runs. The company also does sessions with leadership teams on the impact of running on business and how it can be measured.

The beginnings of Rahul's journey as a runner entrepreneur have been featured in a cover story of *The Week*, a leading Indian magazine, a radio interview by Media Corp 938, a Singaporean Radio channel; 6 bridges, an internet-based site for Indian professionals; and NDTV, a leading Indian TV news channel, among others.

RUNNING and LIVING

UNLEASH YOUR POTENTIAL

RAHUL SALIM VERGHESE

www.visionbooksindia.com

www.visionbooksindia.com

First Published 2015
Reprinted 2016

A Vision Books Original

ISBN 10: 81-7094-939-4
ISBN 13: 978-81-7094-939-8

Published by
Vision Books Pvt. Ltd.
(Incorporating Orient Paperbacks and CARING imprints)
24 Feroze Gandhi Road, Lajpat Nagar 3
New Delhi 110024, India.
Phone: (+91-11) 2984 0821 / 22
e-mail: visionbooks@gmail.com

Printed at
Anand Sons
C 88 Ganesh Nagar, Pandav Nagar Complex
Delhi 110092, India.

Contents

~

Preface

~

"Even after all these years, running continues to amaze me. Mostly in its ability to clarify — to make things OK and bring you back down to earth, even when things are insane; especially, when things are Insane."

– Mark Remy, Executive Editor, runnersworld.com

Life can be tough, full of stress, challenges and worry.

Uncertainty around each corner eats into our optimism. Terrorism, health pandemics, economic ups and downs on a global scale hitherto unimaginable are now frequent news headlines.

"So what can I really manage? Can I?" we ask ourselves.

Layoffs are commonplace, and eat into self-confidence.

Within these larger gloomy umbrellas, perseverance gets hit and ultimately stresses and strains build, and health takes a beating both physically and, more importantly, emotionally and psychologically.

It is no wonder then that we are living in an age where cardiac, diabetic and hypertension issues abound like never before. This makes for a heady cocktail of health problems that have been hitting an ever-wider audience, despite advances in medicine, and even making an appearance at ever-younger ages.

~

Having managed global market research with Motorola for some years, I met, saw, listened to, and observed several consumers around the globe from behind two-way mirrors.

The 40-plus consumers in some large markets, when asked about their "dreams" talked a lot about, "I could have, should have, but at my age and with my health — I have decided not to . . . "

The twenty-five year olds dreamt about becoming a business head or the CEO in their organization, but also wondered at times whether they would be able to make the requisite work-life trade-offs and have the perseverance to move on.

But the six to ten year olds were clear. "I want to have the biggest candy store", or "I will build the best computer game store." For them there are no constraints and the "how to" is the easy part. The dream is already pretty close to reality for them.

That got me wondering if there's something we can do periodically to become five year olds again, to have a dream and the confidence to live it, and live life to its fullest.

~

"I can't imagine living and not running."

– Paula Radcliffe, world champion marathoner

In parallel, I started running accidentally at the end of 2000 while posted in Chicago, and in five months I moved from a semi–couch potato to running 5 kilometres, and in another five months I ran my first-ever marathon in 2001. At the Chicago Marathon I saw myself and other adults become five year olds again at the finish line — exulting, jumping for joy, weeping with the impact of what had been achieved. Running had started fuelling a passion for crossing each barrier, going onwards, achieving, and doing more, like never before. I met world champions, CEOs, doctors, people who had conquered some form of substance abuse, others who had overcome asthma, diabetes, or lost weight and reduced cholesterol, and a few other average and accidental runners like myself, for all of whom now, running was part of their DNA; with the runner's highs, camaraderie and many other reasons for why we like to start our day with a run. I read about the medical and other benefits of running, and then I began to believe that the simple act of running could be the route to get us all to feel like a five year old again. And get us to start living life to the fullest, as we would like to.

And we could be running and living.

And that's when I quit my marketing career of twenty-five years and dreamed of building running into a powerful marketing platform for brands to engage in a fun and innovative way with highly charged communities, and get 200 million people to start running. I do not want to be summarizing my life saying, "I could have, should have, would have . . . " but I want to say, "I did."

So this is a book about living our dreams, in the crazy, fast-paced, and ever-changing and exciting world we live in today. It's about a few of my experiences coupled with wider learning, through reading and talking to doctors, athletes and other sports persons, coaches and, most importantly, thousands of fellow runners over my fifteen short years of running, where my bones have never complained yet about the fifty-one marathons that I have put them through. Running is something simple that I took up by chance. Perhaps you can purposefully decide to take it up tomorrow, and find yourself surprised by the difference it makes to your life, and gain more in a year than I have to date.

> "Running is the greatest metaphor for life, because you get out of it what you put into it."
>
> – Oprah Winfrey, Chicago Marathoner

This is a book about the similarities of life and running, and how through running, you can transform yourself. This book is not about getting you to be an Olympian as the world understands it, but for you to wear your own Olympic medal, in the area you dream about and use running as a tool to get you there.

Like every other human being on this planet, I too have made a gazillion poor choices, had some poor relationships — personal and professional, and perhaps missed several opportunities. But the one thing I definitely did right, was to start running; better late than never. I started at forty. It's made me fitter and more optimistic, and has changed my life.

Here's to you starting running.

And living your life to the fullest, and infecting those around you with the running bug along the way.

~

I am grateful to my wife Jamuna and daughters Diya and Naina for their patience with those early morning alarms and more; for the support of friends, parents, brother, extended family, erstwhile colleagues at Motorola and the running fraternity; and several well wishers including marketing gurus, business heads, entrepreneurs and lawyers, for patiently listening to my rants over the years. Thanks to Evette Cordy for her chapter on running during pregnancy, and to Urmimala Dutt for adding in the dimension of "running beyond the body." Pooja Gandhi laboured to make sense of what I had written and patiently went through each chapter, editing out and editing in. Yasmeen Tayebbhai laboured with love and passion on the cover, and Kapil at Vision Books put it all together and made this happen.

But the first step of getting me on track with Running And Living and entrepreneurship was Joy Ganvik who was my ever supportive boss at Motorola.

Thanks to all of you, I have made a good first step, it's easier from here on.

~

Part 1

~

Personal Transformation

1

~

On Your Marks, Get Set, Dream!

In May 1961, US President John Kennedy put forth a dramatic goal — sending an American safely to the moon and back, before the end of the decade. This was an ambitious, seemingly impossible goal — but it was a public statement of intent that got people roused up, got their minds thinking and resources working. It was a dream that fired the imagination not only of Americans but also the rest of the world, including the Soviets.

"Don't Just Sit There Dreaming! Do Something!!"

You have probably heard this refrain since childhood . . . and perhaps you hear it in your office every other day. And then you snap out of your little mental wander, feeling guilty about doing something horribly wrong! But this book is all about dreaming, and then living your dream.

Psychoanalysts like Sigmund Freud and Carl Jung described dreams as interactions between the unconscious and the conscious, where the unconscious is the dominant force. Dreams have held meaning for the purposes of healing as well as for guidance or divine inspiration. Historically, dreams, or divinations through dreams, have often had powerful influences over cultures. Dreams have been described as psychological reflections of the subconscious, and spiritual messages from gods, or predictions of the future.

"I have a dream," said Martin Luther King, concluding his famous speech in 1963, outlining various aspects of his vision for racial equality. This was such an energizing, uniting, and uplifting message that it provided a positive sense of purpose to huge swaths of peoples across America and, later, several other countries. It got people to think beyond their current seemingly helpless situations, into a future of hope.

~

Running on my treadmill in April 2001, I was delighted at having been able to run thirty minutes without stopping. I dreamt of running a marathon. The Chicago Marathon in October 2001 was what I dreamt about.

"How will you do it? Go for it in 2002 and focus on a good 10k* or a half marathon this year." This was what my colleagues who already ran regularly would tell me. I did not know how I would do it, but I dreamed about it.

---

* A 10-kilometre run.

The subconscious rules our conscious being, and any long-term behavioural change has to originate from the subconscious, otherwise the flesh would be willing but the spirit weak! Fascinating, inspiring, drawing us toward greater deeds than we think we are capable of, stirring the powerful unconscious and unleashing our potential — that's what dreams are about.

~

It was certainly true of my first marathon in 2001.

At the 24-mile mark, I was dog-tired but my subconscious literally pushed me over the finish line. I put it down to all the rigorous training during the preceding five months when I coached myself with positive talk, and my subconscious started seeing me cross that finish line several times over. I'm not sure I can explain it well enough but those last two miles were truly about mind over matter.

That's what a dream does.

It ignites passion.

It provides purpose, and it gives hope and optimism, which make tough times look simple, and makes the challenge exciting.

Dreams do not specify how to get something done, but they can make humans move mountains.

So the power of a dream, whichever way you look at it, should not be underemphasized.

~

During my last corporate assignment with Motorola, I managed global market research for the company's cell phone business. I travelled across the world, and talked to people of varied cultures, directly and indirectly — in stores, in focus groups, *via* questionnaires and on flights — and also during marathons. I started sifting information about dreams and ambitions as I learnt a bit more each day in this big classroom called life.

Some people have dreams that are very operational, short-term and rational:

"I dream about getting a promotion this year."

Others focus on doing something emotionally fulfilling and meaningful:

"I dream that I will help my children be good human beings and stay happy."

But the vast majority do not really have a dream, and when posed the question, respond with a quick, "I dream that I will win a lottery," or "make a million dollars," or . . . .

And when asked what their ambitions are, many of the working 40-plus would respond with, "I could have been the CEO of my organization had I . . . but at my age . . . ," seeming to be resigned to their fate, and wanting to stay content within all their constraints.

The 25-plus state their ambitions of being a business head in five to ten years, but here again many say:

"You know what, I've risen fast, I've tried hard, but *he* has a godfather . . . ,"

and seemingly give up the chase at an early stage.

The tweens, teens and other younger respondents are the most interesting — confident, clear and focused.

"I want to have the biggest candy store in the world so that I can . . . ," or

"I am going to develop the coolest online game that will get people together," or

"I am going to cut my first CD before my next birthday."

They have no constraints and the "how to" is the easy part. For them, the dream is already pretty close to reality.

The interesting thing I found, if I were to generalize, is that the five-year olds had dreams fuelled by, and fuelling, passion. Constraints were no part of their big picture.

The older folk, in contrast, had constraints in their heads, and getting rid of a constraint then potentially became their "operational" dream, far less energizing a dream, than the dream of a five-year old.

Let's All Become Five-Year Olds Again

Let's look at some of our old photographs, of when we were kids, look at children around us and relive some of those moments, and . . . you guessed it — dream! Unbridled, unfettered and undisturbed.

Go for a walk and dream.

Hang out in a spa and dream while you listen to soothing music and get pampered.

Sit and listen to falling rain and nothingness, and dream.

Maybe just take time off and unwind, relax, then gradually rewind to what you really used to enjoy doing, and what you would really like to do, accomplish or experience. You owe it to yourself.

So this is what I have to say.

Don't just rush around doing something all the time, because life can become very routine and you can become an automaton. Take time off, in your very own way, and dream. Get strategic about life. It's *your* life and it's the only certain one you have on this planet.

Don't reach your death-bed thinking, "Oh I could have, would have or should have . . . ," instead of saying with a smile, "I did!!"

Live life to the fullest, rewrite the rules by which you live, unlearn and re-learn constantly and, most importantly, start of by dreaming. That's where it all begins and that's what fuels the fire within.

> "To believe that what has not occurred in history will not occur at all, is to argue disbelief in the dignity of man."– Mahatma Gandhi

In the same vein, you should re-think about yourself, your career, your family and your life.

~

After an MBA from the Indian Institute of Management, Ahmedabad, and twenty-five years of marketing various products and services with Unilever, Nestlé, a small garments company, and then Motorola, I found myself consumed with a passion for running. And that's what got me thinking, "Was there some way to meaningfully fuse my newly awakened passion for running with my 25-year experience in marketing?"

I did not go through this process in a systematic way. Maybe if I had, I would have been clearer and quicker off the blocks. I had participated in about eighteen marathons across the world as I travelled far and wide in my job, I had shaken hands with some world champions, run with thousands of amateur runners like myself, met doctors, venture capitalists, bankers, friends and a whole host of people — bouncing ideas on how I could possibly make a living out of running — knowing I was no Gebrselassie or Usain Bolt.

I then started a website, www.runningandliving.com, in early 2006 goaded by my journalist brother in Hong Kong. This was targeted at the beginner runner, with links to schedules, information, and more. It was a small beginning, and my US $150 investment to set up this site and manage it myself was an experiment well worth every cent. A year later I found myself writing a fortnightly column focused on running and corporate work life, and later a monthly column for a financial newspaper in India, *The Mint.* I started getting emails from readers and visitors on my website, with some statements that were as dramatic as, "You have changed my life!"

Now I am no pastor, preacher, doctor, or healer. So hearing stuff like this was both electrifying and insightful. I got goose bumps as I read these responses and comments from people I had never met. And they made a huge impact on me.

I started thinking how a simple thing like running could have far-reaching benefits spread across the planet, given that it is such an egalitarian pursuit. Most people have run, or can run. It does not cost the earth, does not require coordination with a huge team, and does not need a special playing field. That made me feel good, but the rational question that I, and every sensible person I met, would ask was — "How on earth are you going to make money through this running thing?"

I was convinced that running with its multiple benefits could do great good. My 25 years of marketing and experiencing the world's major marathons and community runs was a good backgrounder to build running as a potent marketing platform for brands, and make it a sustainable pursuit.

Thus began the process of refining my goal and creating a business vision.

I handed in my resignation at Motorola, where my boss was very supportive. What I did know was that my focus was going to be on running, I had a website, I wrote articles on running in a financial daily, and I wanted to start a running magazine. More, I wanted to organize 5- and 10-kilometre fun runs, and run marathons myself — In India, a country of walkers, where runners were still looked upon as a mad subspecies that had not yet discovered the automobile!

So far not a very sensible sounding plan!

Six months later, I realized that publishing a magazine about running was a different kettle of fish and a beast that I wasn't passionate about. I met lots of friends who patiently listened to my raving and ranting about how running could change lives and change the world — bankers, investors, doctors, lawyers, business executives, journalists, and more. I got loads of ideas and inputs to help me sharpen and refine the operational plan of my dream.

And then it dawned on me.

Running is about unleashing potential — that's what it did for me. It broke barriers of different sorts, one by one, enabled discovery at another level, and built self-confidence and optimism with each new broken barrier.

For business, it was a potent way to connect with consumers in a meaningful, fun and engaging manner, and would make strategic sense for a variety of brands and thus make for a superb marketing platform.

After much refining and soul searching, I wrote out our vision statement:

> "We are focused on enabling brands, organizations and individuals to unleash their potential in a fun and engaging manner — *via* running."

Our goal was to get two hundred million people running.

So that's really what I am focused on, and have been for the last several years.

"Two hundred million people? That's crazy! How will you ever measure it?" I have heard many say.

But I said to myself, as I say to them, that you never measure a dream, really. It's way out there, and it drives you. To get two hundred million people to benefit, building a marketing platform, helping fuse my experience with my passion — all of this will certainly force me to think out of the box and do totally different things, differently.

So started the pursuit of my dream. Literally. And I felt like a five-year old again — confident, consumed by my passion, never seeing something as impossible; tough maybe, but impossible? No way!

And to those who rue their fate I would say:

- Don't focus on the fact that you got a C in Math in the last exam, dashing your dream of making it to Harvard. Keep that dream alive and strong. Then, work on alternative paths to get there, focusing on what you need to do to convert your C into an A+. Or perhaps it is an opportunity to review your subject mix and re-examine where your heart lies — and ask yourself again what you would ideally love to do.

- Forget that someone else has been promoted instead of you. Maybe you were not cut out for the role, which possibly required a slightly different set of skills than yours. Or perhaps this is an opportunity to work out your own plan, revisit your dream, or create one if you don't have one yet.

- Forget that your school classmate is a millionaire, and you are without savings, paying out huge mortgages, and clinging to your job. Remember the dream.

- Don't focus on the fact that you have just been downsized. Maybe this is an opportunity to dream of what you really want to do. Technologists have become chefs, and scientists have gone into the field of social work. Always look at your current situation as an opportunity and you will find opportunity knocking your door down.

- If you look at your life through a pessimist's lens you will be surprised by the silence, and will never hear opportunity knock; just the ticking of the clock as time passes on.

Surround yourself physically or metaphorically with thoughts of your childhood or the happiest times you had, and what you perhaps wanted to do when you grew up, and start writing down your dream or dreams.

Take a week off.

Listen to your favourite music and go over what has excited you most in the last few years, what types of magazines you have found yourself picking up and why. And then keep asking yourself why your dream is so exciting, how you can climb another notch in this process, whether you will eventually come out with a vision statement of what you want to achieve, and how much satisfaction you will gain from it. Rewrite it, revise it, junk it, pick it up again — it's like one of those strategy sessions you run for your business, where nothing seems quite perfect. Except, this one is tougher because the stakes are higher. It's about your life.

Perhaps you already have a passion that charges you. Is there a way to laterally shift to an area in your organization that requires that passion? Or, perhaps, move to a different organization, or start something quite different on your own.

Maybe you are clear about what drives you, and can drive you for the next 25 years; if so, that's great.

Or, perhaps, you are like me. During the first 25 years of my working life, things were not so clear. To be honest, I hadn't the foggiest idea of what I really wanted to do, but was coasting along quite happily. This is when you know you have your work cut out for you. It may take some time, while you work in parallel with your current situation, to help define your passion and the dream that you want to pursue.

There are different routes to dreaming that each one of us finds more natural, and that's what we need to do.

I would say to you, perhaps start running a little bit. Think about it if you haven't already, and as you face your boundaries and barriers, it may take you on a journey that will make you feel more positive, somewhat uplifted, and put you in the right frame of mind to dream. I stumbled upon this route by accident — it started on a treadmill. I know there are several other ways to start, but this is perhaps the simplest one I know of.

> "If you have built castles in the air, that is where they should be. Now put foundations under them." – Henry David Thoreau

So what are you waiting for?

Go ahead and start dreaming!

And when you are through, just ask yourself a few questions.

Is it huge?

Does it inspire you?

Does it seem quite out of reach?

Does it sound like heaven?

If it does, you seem to be on to a great dream. You're better off than most on the planet.

Great going!

~

2

~

The Great Barrier Reef

"A pessimist sees the difficulty in every opportunity, an optimist sees the opportunity in every difficulty."

– Winston Churchill

I have never been to Australia's Great Barrier Reef but having seen a few documentaries and films I have often marvelled at how pretty, dangerous and exciting it would be to snorkel and dive there. The Great Barrier Reef has witnessed many a shipwreck over the centuries killing hundreds of sailors, and yet it remains a most popular destination for sightseers, divers, snorkelers and other travellers. So while it is a place that is both dangerous and forbidding, yet once you move beyond the fears you get to enjoy the spectacular diversity and beauty that the reef has to offer.

Many a time we focus on the "great barriers" in life rather than the beautiful "reef" that lies beyond them, and chug along, perhaps unhappily, in a status quo, not daring to step out and try something challenging, something new.

There are two categories of barriers that prevent us from putting on our running shoes. Some of these are internal to us and some are external.

The Internal Barriers

Figure 1: **The Great Barrier Reef — Internal barriers: It's all in the mind**

The internal barriers broadly fall into the following five buckets:

1. **Ill-health:** The worry of being frail, having cardiovascular issues, blood sugar, blood pressure (BP), stress issues and various other major or minor health conditions often

dissuade us from taking the plunge, essentially preventing us from changing the status quo, let alone looking beyond. And then there is the added anxiety caused by some of the half-truths associated with running . . .

- "Running is bad for the knees."
- "It is not good for the heart."

All these issues are what normally make running a non-starter.

2. **Lack of perseverance makes for the next set of road-blocks:**
   - "It's not going to be easy," I have heard people say, "It is tough to start and the first month is very difficult."
   - "So many of my friends have given up. I am not sure I will be able to last that long, so why start."
3. **Pessimism comprises issues like:**
   - "It is just not possible, the whole environment is tough and not meant for someone like me. It's too dusty and hot."
   - "What about the dogs and the heat? I could do this in the US but not in this country," or "In my village but not in this city," etc.
4. **Low self confidence:**
   - "I don't think *I* can do it, I could if I was younger, or as slim as her,"
   - "What will people think when they see me run?"

- "No one here runs ."
- "I can't run in shorts."
- "I don't have the right gear and equipment, people will laugh at me."

5. **"Just no time":**
   - "I am too busy."
   - "I travel a lot."
   - "I have irregular work hours."
   - "I entertain a lot."

Funnily enough, these categories of internal barriers are similar to those that rear up when we are faced with a daunting task at work or in our lives.

So what is your barrier today? Or what has it been for the last several years?

The External Barriers

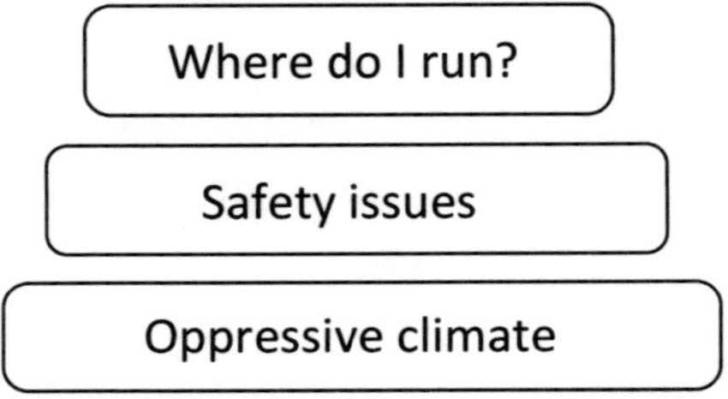

Figure 2: **The Great Barrier Reef — External Barriers: I'm keen to start but it's too tough out there**

Then there are the external barriers, which are several, ranging from, but not limited to, the following:

- The climate is a barrier in many locations: "It's too hot," "It's too cold," "It's too humid," "It's always raining."
- The surroundings and traffic: "It's dirty, too much traffic, too polluted, too noisy."

  Incidentally, this applies to several countries I have run in, especially in Asia, and definitely true for many cities across India.
- "I am worried about stray dogs. It's not safe to run alone."
- "Where do I run? The roads are potholed, no proper trails, no scenic area to run in."

There are several other seemingly credible reasons why one should not run, but let me put down a few things that I have experienced over the years since I started running in India, especially in Delhi, which has a hot summer and a reasonably cold winter, stray dogs, no running paths, no running culture (till 2007), and more. I could safely say that I have run reasonable distances in over 40 countries and 100 cities, and have faced most of the above issues all over the world.

In oppressive and unsafe climes — start with running on a treadmill, at home or in a gym. Listen to music, find some company.

External barriers to running are like the systemic issues we raise as reasons why something cannot be done.

Run in the early mornings since that is when there is low or no traffic. Do the same if you are in a dusty, dry area — the dust is more settled on the ground at that time, so it is much easier and healthier to run then.

If you begin running outdoors, join a running group, chat about the weather issues, or whatever, while you run with the safety of numbers. Dogs also get intimidated when they see ten runners instead of two juicy legs to bite into!

> "Free your mind, and your feet will follow."
> – Kevin Nelson, *The Runner's Book of Daily Inspiration*

Over time as the joys of running kick in, you will find yourself starting to run right from outside your door even if it is none too exciting a route.

But you must start sensibly and follow a schedule, check with your doctor before you set out, and don't ever overdo it.

> "We all have dreams. But in order to make dreams come to reality, it takes an awful lot of determination, dedication, self-discipline, and effort."– Jesse Owens

Busting Those Barriers

We moved from Singapore to Chicago in April 2000. Summer in Chicago was fantastic — music, food, festivals, and more. And then came our first Chicago winter. It got a little grey and cold quite early in the evening — read "pitch black" — and minus 30 with wind chill, at 5 p.m. You often don't get to see too many people around. In the Chicago suburbs you see a neighbour only after the snowmen have melted. That was when I understood why polar bears sensibly hibernate.

I decided to turn to my newly-bought treadmill. I thought of running because it was a cold winter and I was trying to pass thirty minutes of time. So my motivation was neither fitness related nor a physical goal. I found that I could run 2.5 miles in thirty minutes with a few walking breaks, which was pretty good in my book.

When I was not travelling for work, I also began skiing every weekend. I had bought myself a pair of 180 cm straights. Not the best skis for a beginner but they cost US $30, which made it an easy decision. During my first lesson I stumbled and slipped up the rope tow and came down slithering in an ungainly fashion. Looking around I could see tiny kids skiing confidently like professionals. I grew a thick skin, so to speak, and tried to make sure I fell well, and did not hurt myself when I fell. Most of all I learned not to care two hoots about what people around might think. In this, I had to overcome a huge mental barrier. Soon I found many other beginners of my age group, and I discovered that I wasn't too bad compared to many of them.

Back home in our basement with the noisy treadmill, by April I found myself finally managing 3.5 miles in thirty minutes — without stopping! I pumped the air with my fist, delighted with where I had reached. It was a huge achievement for me. I had never imagined that I would be able to run more than five kilometres without stopping. Looking back, I felt that I, the accidental runner, had definitely broken a barrier here.

On the ski slopes, meanwhile, I was picking up confidence. I was able to stop and turn without bumping into anyone or anything. For the first time I moved from the bunny slope for beginners to the green slope, which was three times longer yet still quite gentle. Then, somehow, on my third trip I decided to go down the blue slope, which is the next grade after the beginner green slopes. Despite taking many a toss I managed to pick myself up with as much grace as I could muster, while some folks in the chair lifts looked on in amusement.

Next weekend, just before setting out from home I decided to come down a black slope, one of the toughest grades of slopes. Not the most sensible thing for a forty-year-old three-time skier to try out, but I like to claim that adventure is in my blood. So I went up the ski lift and stood at the top of the black diamond slope. I watched a few seasoned skiers go down gracefully. After a lot of self-encouragement and bravado, I found myself engaged in trying to slither down with all body parts intact. And I did! I may have looked more like I was slip-sliding rather than skiing, but I was ecstatic when I made it down. A major barrier was broken! After that I always returned to get better, improve my technique, and learn. There was no fear any more.

As you break barriers one by one, it builds self confidence and optimism — that is the greatest benefit.

Myths about Running: Some Half-Truths and Some Facts

Running has been subjected to diverse research over the last forty years, longitudinally, with matched samples across twins, gender, race, climate and altitude. Running has been investigated by universities and hospitals, sports medicine specialists, orthopaedic surgeons, theologists and multitudes of other professionals and earned its share of critics and evangelists in good measure.

The good news is that our understanding of the need for regular exercise, such as running, in our increasingly sedentary and highly pampered lifestyles is vastly enhanced.

Myth

Running is bad for the joints.

This is the most widespread one.

In fact, evidence suggests that running might even have some protective effect on the joints. Increased muscle strength and constant motion preserves the biomechanics of the joint. The critical areas to focus on are:

- Appropriate running shoes based on whether you are flat-footed, high arched, or neutral arched.

- Pronation, the natural side-to-side movement of the foot as you walk or run.
- Checking and improve your running style.

To a large extent technology has helped overcome some of the challenges involved. "Very often, inappropriate running shoes or running style cause foot pain, which gradually tends to creep up the skeletal system to the ankles, then knees, hips, and ultimately, the lower back," explains Dr SKS Marya.*

Here is an expert view on the subject:

> "In a well-known long-term study conducted at Stanford University, California, researchers tracked nearly 1,000 runners (active members of a running club) and non-runners (healthy adults who didn't have an intensive exercise regimen) for 21 years. None of the participants had arthritis when the study began, but many of them developed the condition over the next two decades. When the Stanford team tabulated the data, published in the Archives of Internal Medicine in 2008, it found that the runners' knees were no more or less healthy than the non-runners' knees. And it didn't seem to matter how much the runners ran. 'We have runners who average 200 miles a year and others who average 2,000 miles a year. Their joints are the same,' says James Fries, a

* Dr. SKS Marya, MS, DNB, MCh (UK), FICS, Vice Chairman on the Max Healthcare Board of Directors & Chairman — Orthopaedics, in Delhi, India.

> professor emeritus of medicine at Stanford and the leader of the research group. The study also found that runners experienced less physical disability and had a 39% lower mortality rate than the non-runners.
>
> – *Time,* December 25th, 2009

An excerpt from a study four years later showed even more positive support for running being "good" for the skeletal system.

> "The notion that running causes wear and tear on the joints that could spur arthritis makes some intuitive sense. But if anything, running probably offers protection from osteoarthritis, says Paul Williams, an exercise scientist at Lawrence Berkeley National Laboratory, USA, who leads the National Runners' Health Study and the National Walkers' Health Study. These projects have enlisted almost 90,000 runners and walkers and followed them since the studies began. Williams calculated rates of osteoarthritis and hip replacement among participants in his studies and found that runners were approximately half as likely as walkers to develop osteoarthritis or need a hip replacement. Furthermore, runners who ran the most had the lowest risk of osteoarthritis.
>
> – *Washington Post,* August 12th, 2013.

By the way, running also causes you to lose weight, helps strengthen calf and thigh muscles and therefore also reduce pressure on the joints in your normal day-to-day life.

Truth

The predictable, repetitive motion of running makes the care of the feet and joints for runners a much easier task to manage than for many other sports, especially as we age.

Due to their random and high impact movements and angular shifts and lunges, tennis, squash and soccer tend to take an inordinate toll on the knees and ankles over the years. This leaves the three aerobic sports of swimming, cycling and running as activities that you could potentially continue into your older years.

Myth

Long distance running is for young people.

Fauja Singh ran in the 2011 London Marathon when he was a hundred. Dr Ashis Roy ran his 114th marathon in Gurgaon that my company had organized in 2012 at 80.

And both these men light up like five-year olds when they talk about running.

So you can happily strike off the myth that long-distance running is for younger folks and that running is bad for your body.

Truth

Walking is not good enough.

Another study done in the UK clearly focused on the need for regular vigorous activity rather than just moderate physical activity on a regular basis.

The centenarian Fauja Singh in a long distance run

India is known to be a country of walkers, but is the emergent global capital of cardiac, diabetic, and hypertension-related issues — not something to be proud of.

A study in the UK of 2,401 twins found that a sedentary lifestyle raises the risk of a range of problems from heart disease to cancer and appears to play a key role in the ageing process. According to the researchers, exercise lowers the risk of problems such as heart disease, diabetes and some forms of cancer, especially breast and colon.

"It is not just walking around the block. It is really working up a sweat," says Tim Spector, a genetic epidemiologist who led the afore-mentioned study.

Truth

Do you want to live longer?

A study from Kings College, London in 2007 stated the following:

> "Exercise may hold the key to youth; people who keep fit are up to nine years biologically younger than those who do not."

The study found that people who exercised vigorously three hours each week were biologically nine years younger than people who exercised less than fifteen minutes. Slim people are not necessarily fit and a slightly heavier person who exercises regularly is likely to be fitter and healthier than a thin person who is sedentary.

This study, which adjusted for body weight, smoking, economic status, and physical activity at work, also, highlighted that "moderate exercise for one-and-a-half hours each week provided a four-year advantage."

So do you want a four-year advantage or do you want to be biologically nine years younger? Either way, hit the ground running!

Truth

Running is the simplest way to achieve this.

I am focusing here on running because it is within the reach of every person — it can be done at any time and in any

The Case of Jim Fixx

Jim Fixx is the father of running in the US. He popularised running, and evangelised the many benefits of regular running. He also died at the age of 52.

But his father had died of a heart attack at the age of 43 and Jim himself was born with an enlarged heart. He started running when he was 35 years old, weighing in at 110 kgs and smoking ten packs of cigarettes a day. Ten years later he was sixty pounds lighter and had quit smoking. He himself acknowledged many a time that had he not started running, he most likely would have not lived to celebrate his 40th birthday.

place, at home on a treadmill, or outside on a road or in a park. Neither does it require any major facilities nor expensive club memberships.

Simply put, I would argue that running is the easiest everyday route to get us to go beyond the great barriers and experience the beauty of the reef — and it does not require a huge amount of money. Anyone from a CEO to a newspaper vendor, from a nursery student to a grandma can do it.

Truth

Anything done improperly and in excess can take a toll.

The point is, if you are aware of the issues you will make adjustments in order to minimize them; balance things out, while focusing on the benefits. The same holds true for running. Many myths abound, which are based on outdated information. You need to know how to start, look at your lifestyle, a decent schedule, and not overdo it. The same is true about running — you overdo it, ramp up too fast in your new found exuberance, or go in for a long distance race, or run in an unfamiliar climate without training, and you could be headed for trouble.

~

Benefits of Running are Multi-Dimensional and Life-Changing, Almost Miraculous

There are hundreds of studies done across the world on runners, which have found seemingly magical benefits of running. Some of them are listed below:

- Running gives you a healthier heart:
  - More of high density lipoprotein (HDL), or good cholesterol and lower levels of LDL, or bad cholesterol.
  - Stronger heart muscles and the attendant lowered pulse rate.
  - More flexible arteries.
- Running reduces stress levels, blood pressure and hypertension.
- Running burns blood sugar more efficiently and helps manage Type-2 diabetes.
- Running overcomes jet lag.

You may find it hard to believe, but I found running a great way to overcome jet lag. I used to travel around 200,000 miles a year, often landing eight time zones away. At late night work discussions I would often find my local colleagues dozing off, while I would be bright and alert. I put this down to my early morning runs after checking into the hotel. Those thirty minutes would re-set my clock and get me charged up for the day ahead in the new time zone.

I was heading to Rio De Janeiro to run in the Rio Marathon. A hectic work week in California and Brazil with a climactic marathon in Rio was made possible by sound sleep at night, all thanks to the morning runs. No melatonin for me. I have found this to be the simplest way to manage jet lag over the last decade and a half.

Equally, a vigorous, even tiring workout has actually been known to energize and de-stress, so much so that some doctors have used it to treat clinically depressive patients. The endorphins (endogenously created morphine) released during the run get the runner on a high. It's the only legally approved way of going on a trip and having your parents say proudly, "Look, my son is really tripping. He seems really high today! He's actually behaving like a five-year old!"

- Running reduces the incidence of catching the common cold and keeps the flu at bay. The only problem with this is that it eliminates yet another possible excuse that you used for skipping work when you wanted to. Now no longer.

- Running helps you get over sinusitis. I can personally vouch for this. While based in Singapore for four years, I came down with acute sinusitis for which I had to undergo a minor surgery to drain two cavities, with a plug in my right ear for a year after that. Once I started running I found my sinuses were drained with the first bit of sweat, much like a steam inhalation would do, and I have never looked back.
- Running reduces the incidence of colon and breast cancer. Both have been found to be much lower in people who run.
- Running slows down brain degeneration. Brain atrophy to a certain extent is a normal phenomenon in old age. However, it is documented in scientific studies that running causes brain cells to regenerate and keeps several degenerative illnesses of the brain in abeyance. Scientific studies have also shown that running improves memory.
- "Running provides a direct benefit to the musculo-skeletal system," according to leading orthopaedic surgeon Dr SKS Marya, who is a specialist in knee replacement in India. Here's how:

    1. **Bones:** Running increases the mineral density of the bones and reduces the risk of osteoporosis with age. It has been found that the average bone mineral density

in the thigh is 5% higher in runners than their non-running companions, and 8% higher than those who did not exercise at all, making them less susceptible to fractures following minor falls.

2. **Joints:** Running builds and strengthens muscle tissue, especially in the lower limbs. Increased muscle strength also provides a protective cover to the joints. Current evidence suggests that a moderate level of running does not increase the risk of osteoarthritis of hip and knee for healthy people. It is unclear if long-distance running causes the hip and knee joints to deteriorate.

My friends in the corporate world warn me that I should now stop running, since I'm no spring chicken at 50-plus and this is what I tell them:

> "You probably already have lower back pain given your posture and travel. In addition, I am guessing carpal tunnel syndrome, various repetitive stress injuries, issues with hyperacidity due to improper meal times, and borderline diabetes too. Entertaining clients or colleagues, in addition to conference calls must be keeping you up at night, besides adding a bit of stress and tension. Spondylitis, high cholesterol and mild cardiac issues must have taken root by now. But you take it all in your stride and are proud of how much you are putting in to climb the corporate ladder; you carry your ailments with a sense of pride, almost as a badge of

honour. Your family life probably bears the brunt of most of your stress and tension, right?"

Divorced by 40 and dead by 45, is this really the way you planned to live your life?

The point is, if you are aware of the problems you owe it to yourself to adjust accordingly and minimize them, and to balance things out. Often the more comfortable we get doing something that is not really positive, exciting or challenging, the more resistant we get to change, despite feeling intrinsically dissatisfied and unhappy.

"I am waiting for my retirement plans to fructify," or "I'm waiting for our second child to get married," are some typical refrains. But then what? Most likely, when you retire, the refrain will then shift to, "I am too old now or I have health issues," or back to the familiar, "I could have, should have . . ." syndrome and back over the loop again.

"I Have No Time to Run — I Am Just Too Busy"

> "Those who think they have no time for bodily exercise will sooner or later have to find time for illness." – Edward Stanley

What Edward Stanley says is true. I have heard many people say that they don't need to exercise because they are slim and feel fit and healthy. Being slim, as noted earlier, is good but it does not mean that you are healthy, or that you do not need to exercise. It is as absurd as saying that a fat person does not need to eat.

Just go ahead and start today. It's actually much easier than you think.

Presidents of several nations run, captains of industry run, and so do others. Are you busier than them? You need to make the time for things that are important to you. Don't be the first to arrive and the last to leave the party. Have one drink less than your normal quota. Go to sleep thirty minutes sooner and get up thirty minutes earlier four days a week. I found this to be the only "my time" during the day with no cell phone, emails and other distractions, time which also enables me, if I want, to plan my day, think about upcoming meetings, and any complicated issues to be dealt with.

Move Beyond the Barrier, Enjoy the Reef

Get a deeper meaning of life and enjoy it to the fullest. Don't just swim on the surface of the sea, Dive and get below, and you'll be amazed at the views and opportunities that open up.

To give you another perspective, let me share a few quotes from some people who started running at the frequent runs hosted by the venture I started in 2007:

> "I loved every moment of the run and actually ran most of the 5 kilometres . . . hopefully next

time over, I will say that I ran all of the 5 kilometres."

– Nanni, first-time runner who is a leader at an NGO.

~

"I did the 5-kilometre run today and had an amazing time." – Amit

~

"This was my first run and I really enjoyed it . . . although I must mention that it really required a lot of will power to run in this cold weather."

– Ravi

~

"It was indeed a fantastic start for the day . . . and I have gained a lot of stamina with these runs. I am no longer the last one to finish . . . and yes the group brings in a lot of positivity and enthusiasm . . . It's a dream transition for me . . . from a walking person . . . I have become a runner" – Ruchika

~

"I managed to complete the 5k (5-kilometre run) last Saturday, running non-stop without a single break. That was some achievement for me personally and I am proud of it. It inspires me enough to take a shot at the 10k in the August 10 Freedom Run in Gurgaon."

– Dhiraj, a professional

~

"I ran in today's run. I am 27, unfit and totally mortified at the thought of running. However, through a group heard about the runs you organize. I enjoyed the experience, I enjoyed running. In fact, all day I had the feeling that one gets when you are just falling in love with someone. For couch potatoes of the likes of me, it could very well be life-altering." – Neha, a banker

~

Now that is quite something, I am sure you would agree.

Celebrate each small win and talk about the barriers you encountered and crossed, or broke along the way, when you talk to a friend — it will propel you onwards.

The multicoloured clownfish, the corals, the life under water you never imagined, a totally different world, vibrant and ever changing awaits you, out there at the reef.

> "To get to the finish line, you'll have to try lots of different paths." – Amby Burfoot

Go on . . . go past the barrier and enjoy the reef, because now you are beyond constraints — you can start dreaming again.

~

3

~

Why on Earth!

"The only reason I would take up jogging is so that I could hear heavy breathing again."

– Erma Bombeck

Okay, so maybe the incredibly funny Erma Bombeck's reasoning would get many people running. But if you aren't wired like her, perhaps the following is going through your head:

> "Now why would I ever want to run? Aren't there other ways, more fun ways, to go out and dream and break barriers? I could see a nice movie, listen to a great motivational talk, play tennis, swim, or try some jazz dancing or whatever."
>
> "And this guy seems cuckoo in any case . . . he quit his job to run and to get others to start running!"

The advantages that running has over all these and most other activities are manifold:

- Running is both an individual as well as a group activity.
- It can be done indoors or outdoors.
- You can run in hotel gyms during your travel days or during early mornings in a park to energize your entire day.
- It can be a long distance run or a short speed run, or even a restful, lazy warm-up, or perhaps a fun run on the beach while on vacation with your spouse and kids, a tougher run in the hills, a brisk run with your dog, or an exercise outing for the entire family. Additionally, you can mix it up with any of the other activities that fit in with your lifestyle.

Moreover, running is a simple activity wherein you can push yourself to the limit by striving for better speed, by increasing the distance you run, or adding steep uphill slopes into your training routine, and feel the crisp breeze on your face, in your hair, or the moisture-laden winds gently pushing you along as you run. Some people like measurements and can instantly check their progress as they monitor the time taken for a given distance — a loop around the park or a track; while others like to hang loose. Some like to run outdoors with an iPod; others like to run early in the morning and hear birds chirping; while yet others like to run in a group and chat, a bit like golf.

This is one activity where five-year olds and 70-year olds can have fun side by side. Not as spectators sipping sugary colas and gorging on potatoes in some form or the other, but as active participants. It is an activity in which you can be a cheerleader and a participant at the same time. You can be alone, or with colleagues or family. You can think about your plans for a specific meeting during the day, or introspect about your life goals . . . and perhaps stumble upon your dream!

> "Hey this running thing is beginning to sound a little bit like life, and perhaps they are quite intertwined in some way, metaphorically."

I hope this is what you are thinking.

The Key to Life

A few years ago I came across a short but wonderful video clip on YouTube by actor Will Smith, after he won the 2005 Kids Choice awards, about the keys to life.

"Running and reading," he claims, "are the keys to life. When you are running there is a little person who talks to you and says, 'I'm tired, my lungs are going to pop, there is no way I can possibly continue,' and you want to quit. Now if you learn how to defeat this person when you're running, you will learn how to not quit when things get hard in life." Google it and watch the video, it's simple and makes the point.

October 7, 2001, Chicago Marathon: 20-Mile Marker

It was my first-ever marathon and the going was really tough. I had done only a single 20-mile run before and all the books had assured me that the adrenaline, crowds and atmosphere would get me through the last 6 miles and 385 yards. That day I experienced what Will Smith was talking about.

"Come on, man — what are you doing to yourself?" said the little man in my head. We had just crossed back onto Halsted Avenue, and were set to cross the river. Then the underpass with the train lines above and a left turn got us to Cermak Road, and I knew China Town was near.

"Okay, okay, just another 10 kilometres," I thought, "and I get to a nice chilled beer, meet up with my wife, kids, parents and cousins at the finish line."

"You're looking good, runners! You guys are heroes!" shouted people all along the route. The energy of the crowd was inspiring, as also were the other slower runners who were in the middle of the pack just as I was.

"You shouldn't be doing this to yourself," continued the little man. "If you wanted to be part of the Chicago Marathon experience, you should have been on the side of the road cheering others on." I had not thought of quitting but now I wondered when the pain would be over. What would I tell my friends and family if for whatever reason I could not finish? "Perish the thought!"

The author running the Chicago Marathon

"I've done this before — only nine kilometres left and that is less than six miles, just what I would do almost every Thursday around Buffalo Grove and Aptakisic roads next to our house. And now there are a bunch of folks cheering me on."

From up ahead the lion dancers, drums and dancing could be heard and would soon be visible.

And then I took a walk break.

I flipped out my camera and took pictures of myself and of the volunteers who were handing out water and energy drinks.

Here at Mile 24, none of us runners were looking much good and there were barely any folks cheering us.

The runners of the Chicago Marathon have taken over the city's streets!

Suddenly one spectator started shouting, "This is a marathon, you cannot walk; get up and move it. You have to run to the finish," and that, I think, jolted me out of my stupor. I was tired, in pain, walking was tough, running was even tougher — but stopping was not an option. That shout killed the "little man" in my head. I thought to myself, "He's right. Can't walk now, must run. The finish will happen faster. I have to finish. I have to be running strong at the finish, I have to be smiling at the finish."

I started hobbling and stumbling, and then running again. I suddenly started feeling stronger. My legs were not aching any more. I passed a church that had a banner up for the marathoners: "Rejoice, for the end is nigh," and with that I finished my first marathon in 4 hours and 32 minutes, with a smile on my face.

Running, after turning 40, had enabled me to start defeating this "little man" inside my head.

Subsequently, several times at work or in life when confronted with something impossible that made me balk and think "No way", I would step back and say to myself, "This looks tough, but let me try and figure out a way to go ahead . . . I know it is possible."

Like Will Smith, I too would say that running is a basic key to life.

> Once we start applying to life what we learn in the classroom of running, magic happens.

I started noticing quite a few things happening to me as I got into running. I started sleeping earlier. I changed my schedule from essentially running in the evenings to running in the mornings. Whenever possible, I started running outdoors. Then I got hooked to the challenge and strove to improve my speed and stamina. And that got me reading, talking to, and observing other runners . . . and learning. I realized that I had to make my body more flexible and that I must also do some weight training. I ate better, more regularly and better quality food — fewer French-fries and more of roasted and baked foods, less cola and beer, and a bit more of fresh juice . . . the list went on. I realised that I was able to focus more sharply when needed, and could look at different ways of approaching an issue that earlier had seemed too tough to resolve.

Over time, in many subtle ways, running was changing my lifestyle for the better.

Some magic was at work . . . .

The Runner's High

The runner's high was finally measured in a lab in Germany some years ago. Dr. Henning Boecker, who led the team of scientists, conducted various tests that confirmed that exercise does, in fact, cause endorphins (endogenously produced morphine) to be released in the brain. This acts on two fronts — reducing pain perception and improving the sense of well being. "It's this flood of endorphins that results in mood changes, such as euphoria and the famed 'runner's high.' "

Just think of it. That endorphin machine is just a pair of legs, or in the case of Oscar Pistorius of South Africa, who amazed the world in the London Olympics, just a pair of stumps. He was born with a problem in his bones below his knees leading to a double amputation. He went on to become a truly fast runner and an inspirational athlete.

However, there is a little something else that is required for this "high" and that is will power, because you need to keep going for a bit in order to get a sufficient endorphin release. The "bit" varies from person to person but normally it needs at least 45 minutes or so of running.

> "When you run in the morning, you gain time in a sense. It's like stretching 24 hours into 25. You may need to sleep less and get up earlier, but if you can get by that, running early seems to expand the day."
>
> – Fred Lebow, founder of the New York City Marathon

So that's why you may want to check out where running could take you, and it may take you way beyond what you had imagined possible on earth. And instead of asking yourself, "Why on earth am I running?" you may end up saying, "What in heaven's name took me so long to start?"

So, Why on Earth?

- Keep the big dream right in front of you and think of your life on this planet and what you can do.
- Surround yourself with inspirational stories that seem impossible.
- Stay around positive people and you may be surprised when you begin to see more possibilities than obstacles.
- Perhaps go out for a short run.
- Think about beating that "little man" and celebrate each little win.

That will give you the answer for people who ask you why on earth you are running. The smile and glow on your face will say it all.

4

~

Starting Pains

"Ability is what you are capable of doing. Motivation determines what you do. Attitude determines how well you do it."

– Lou Holtz

Starting is tough, painful, but beyond that the beauty starts unfurling, bit-by-bit.

The first run and the first week are always the toughest: physically, mentally and, shall I add, emotionally.

"I ran yesterday so maybe I'll do the next run after a few days."

"I'm slim in any case, so I should be fine if I run again only next week."

There goes the "little man" in your head — again.

Two days into running on my newly-purchased treadmill I found my legs aching like crazy. The 40-year-old calves and quadriceps had been rediscovered after hibernation since my college days. They throbbed with pain and fuelled many long speeches from the discouraging "little man." I was rediscovering a principle from school physics that the coefficient of starting friction is higher than the coefficient of sliding friction — even though I hadn't reached the second part (sliding friction).

There are starting pains when you join a new company, or move to a new city, or country; so also with any new activity like running. I soon realized that it is very easy to lose your way when you start something new, especially if you do not have serious focus and commitment towards it.

In the beginning I found running to be a bit of a bore, so I tried a Sony MP3 player while on the treadmill. I tried a boom box, too, as I found I was buying and thinking of gadgets to keep myself energized and excited while running on the rubber belt. However, it remained a lonely task, and after the first two or three weeks, I found myself going down to the basement and doing the 30-minute routine reluctantly as if it were a medical prescription.

"Go back a little to leap further." – John Clarke

I had run a maximum of three-and-a-half miles before foolishly announcing to family, friends and colleagues that I was going to run the Chicago Marathon in October 2001.

Having done that, I then bought a book and read the introduction, which can be paraphrased into something like this:

> "Congratulations on your decision to run a marathon. By now you would have run several 5k races, and upped the mileage to many 10k races, you must have even run at least one half marathon and know what it takes to go beyond. Now you are poised to get to where less than 0.1% of the population has gone." – *The Full Marathon*.

I gulped. Perhaps I had bought the wrong book; marathons seemed designed for Olympians. Or was I just making a mistake in trying to run a full marathon in my first year? I decided to glance at the first week's schedule:

June 4: Rest. "That was easy," I said to myself.

June 5: 4 miles. "A bit of a stretch, but I can manage it," I thought.

June 6: 3 miles. "Piece of cake."

June 7: 2.5 miles. "Getting easier!"

June 8: Rest. "Hey, this is really easy."

June 9: 45-minute outdoor run. A little tough, because this would be the first time in six months I would run outdoors.

June 10: 14 miles. "Whoa! No way — impossible! This MUST be a typo!"

I actually did manage to run fourteen miles in two-and-aquarter hours, and since this was an afternoon run in the Chicago summer, it was much hotter than I ever expected. Also, I had rather stupidly not carried a water bottle thinking it a useless appendage and extra weight to carry. I soon paid the price for this, with my tongue hanging out like a dog's in summer. I was running in and out of a McDonald's wherever I saw one, and whizzing by the water fountains.

> "The trouble with jogging is that by the time you realize you're not in shape for it, it's too far to walk back." – Franklin P. Jones

But at the end of the fourteen-mile torture I actually felt like a hero; I felt I could accomplish anything! I was so much more self-assured than when I ran 5 kilometres for the first time on the treadmill. Now in one week I had run four times that, and it was the longest distance I had ever run in my life. Impossible! Amazing!! I was dreaming!!! Anything was definitely possible now.

Sometimes when we start off, we think we know everything, and we experience the starting pains from a lack of listening to those who are better informed.

A few weeks later, while continuing training for my maiden marathon, I did my first long run of 18 miles (29 kilometres) starting from my friend's home in my regular cotton T-shirt and socks. Once again, I paid the price for it. I was sweating like mad, my feet were wet with sweat, and my T-shirt was soaked. Ten miles into my run I could feel a blister and, soon, a couple of them on each foot. The T-shirt was scraping the skin on my chest. My feet were getting more and more painful but I didn't have the courage to unlace my shoes to have a look. By now it was pitch dark and I still had many miles to reach home. I bit my lip and carried on. Once home, I discovered a blister within a blister on one foot, jumped into a warm tub, and screamed in pain when the water touched my nipples. They weren't bleeding but had been cut and the warm water and the sweat stung like crazy.

I remembered the sales rep at the athletic store trying to persuade me to buy running socks and dry-fit T-shirts, all of which I'd thought were just expensive sales gimmicks. I had refused to pay 20 USD for a T-shirt and 6 USD for a pair of running socks, thinking I had comfortable cotton equivalents.

Starting pains, really painful ones, had taught me a lesson in humility. I swore never to ignore what I had read in books and what I had learnt from sales advisors in athletic stores. I realized that I had to first unlearn and then re-learn. Running was beginning to teach me the basics of continuous learning, where sometimes we also have to take a leap of faith.

~

Three years later back in India, in Gurgaon, I was a running convert and an addict, but had to face a yet different set of starting pains. There were stray dogs on the roads, traffic was a mess starting at 7 a.m., it was really dusty, definitely not scenic at all, and worst of all — NO ONE RAN! People looked at me as if I was from another planet. So I started running outdoors early morning after walking my daughters to the school bus stop. It was beautiful in the mornings, not too hot, the dust not yet swirling around but a bit moist with dew, even if there was some traffic. I would occasionally get to glimpse a peacock as it strutted across the road. The dogs would generally be asleep, but I started carrying a stick to try and act tough if a few started chasing after me. On one of my trips back to Chicago I got an electronic remote dog trainer device that was supposed to emit frequencies to scare dogs into submission. I found that the dogs in Gurgaon were either hard of hearing or that the US solutions were too mild for them; so down the drain went yet another gadget that I had proudly bought!

> "The miracle isn't that I finished. The miracle is that I had the courage to start."
>
> – John Bingham, marathoner and writer

What John Bingham says is so true. This does not relate to running a marathon alone, but to any task that seems insurmountable when you start off, but which you finish by breaking into manageable bits. You can then look back with satisfaction, once it has been achieved.

I would like to offer a simple plan for you to check out; one that seems to have done well for some couch potatoes and also for several walkers who had never run for the previous twenty to thirty years, but who have now started running 5-kilometre runs.

Check out the 7-week schedule in Table 4.1 for walkers.

Table 4.1: Seven-Week Schedule for Beginner Walkers

Week	Monday	Tuesday	Wednesday	Thursday	Friday	Saturday	Sunday
1	Rest	Easy walk 30 minutes	Walk +1x100 m run	Easy walk 30 minutes	Rest	Brisk walk 45 minutes	1 hour walk + 2x200 m jog
2	Rest	Easy walk 30 minutes	Walk +2x100 m runs	Easy walk 30 minutes	Rest	Brisk walk 45 minutes	1 hour Walk + 3x200 m jog
3	Rest	Easy walk 30 minutes	Walk +3x100 m runs	Easy walk 30 minutes	Rest	Brisk walk 45 minutes	1 hour jog / walk
4	Rest	Easy walk 40 minutes	Walk +3x100 m runs	Easy walk 30 minutes	Rest	Brisk walk 45 minutes	45 mins jog / walk
5	Rest	Easy walk 30 minutes	Walk +1x100 m runs	Easy walk 30 minutes	Rest	Brisk walk 45 minutes	45 mins jog / walk
6	Rest	Easy walk 30 minutes	Walk +2x100 m runs	Easy walk 30 minutes	Rest	Brisk walk 45 minutes	1 hour jog / walk
7	Rest	Easy walk 30 minutes	Walk +3x100 m runs	Easy walk 30 minutes	Rest	Brisk walk 45 minutes	30 min jog

(© 2008, Running and Living Infotainment.)

Notes

Rest: Keep your feet up from an exercise perspective. Do some slow stretches of the neck and shoulder, touching the toes, etc.

Easy walk: Keep up a pace at which you can converse normally with your walking partner.

Walk + 100m runs: Walk for 10 to 15 minutes and then run approximately 100 metres as fast as you can. Don't worry about the pace. You should be out of breath at the end of that. Then walk for 10 to 15 minutes, catch your breath, keep up the rhythm, and repeat the sequence as many times as required.

Brisk walk: Walk at a pace that makes you break into a sweat.

Easy jog/walk: Walk at a brisk pace and when you feel up to it, convert to a slow jog for a while and then revert to a brisk walk. Convert back to a slow jog once you feel up to it and repeat as many times as you want. You set the pace and the frequency, but don't overdo it. For beginner runners, an easy jog does not mean you cannot take walking breaks. Take walking breaks in between, catch your breath and then resume, but remember — keep the pace down.

Walk +200m jogs: Walk for 5-10 minutes and jog for 200 metres at a comfortable pace (not a sprint!) and then repeat as required.

Jog: Try and maintain a slow and steady pace; you may want to vary the pace in between for variety.

Tempo jog: Go slow for the first ten minutes, then pick up the pace for the middle third of the session, and slow down for the final third.

Like anything in life, ease into the routine gradually, consult your doctor if required, and listen to your body. Don't let machismo take over. And then you may find these basic principles can be applied to your work and to managing your workload:

- Never try and do the same thing repeatedly if you are trying to improve.
- Look at a holistic build-up and focus on different weak links.
- Do not work to exhaustion but work towards a build-up scientifically and sensibly, so that come the big day, you are ready to be firing on all cylinders.
- Rest adequately.
- And . . . you can write in your very own set of learnings.

Minimize Starting Pains

- Keep your shoes and running gear by the side of your bed before you go to sleep.
- Try and get a friend to keep you company so that peer pressure brings both of you to the starting line for the first two weeks.
- Don't overdo anything. Remember that the initial pain is "good" pain.

- Stay focused on your goal and the starting pains begin to fade.
- If you want, carry your music, or listen to the birds, or chase the dogs.
- When you're feeling down, tell yourself that if millions of people have started running, so can you.

And you will.

~

5

~

A Pregnant Pause? Never

by Evette Cordy

(Evette is a very talented market researcher from Australia, who worked with Taylor Nelson Sofres while I was at Motorola in Chicago and Delhi. We were working together on some large projects when we discovered our common passion for running, though I must admit that she was a champion runner! When I was writing this book she had just had a baby boy, and I asked her to share her experiences of running during pregnancy. So here goes, from Evette.)

Sometimes, personal circumstances cross your path to put seemingly huge obstacles in your way as you seek to ambitiously hurtle on, but are they really obstacles? Generally, you come out happier and wiser from the experience, enabling you to better multi-task along your journey to living your dream, because life isn't one dimensional — it would be so boring if it were!

Congratulations! You have just learned that you are pregnant . . . and you want to continue running. Go for it!

When I first found out I was pregnant, I searched for sources to tell me it was okay to keep running. Mostly, I encountered a variety of myths and misconceptions about running during pregnancy:

"You are still running, you can't possibly be pregnant!"

"If you keep running, your baby will get brain damage from all the bouncing up and down."

"If you run when you are pregnant you will pee in your pants."

"You will get stretch marks from your tummy jiggling around."

Scientific research on the effects of running during pregnancy, however, highlights the benefits, both physiological and psychological.

During pregnancy, blood volume goes up by as much as 40 per cent and resting heart rate rises by as much as fifteen beats.

I discovered I was pregnant in Mexico during a five-day mini-break amidst a five-week overseas work jaunt. "Being pregnant is not going to stop me running," I announced to my husband. "In *Sex and the City*, Charlotte ran while she was pregnant."

I was half-serious, half-joking. I had been consistently running five days a week for the past few months and hoped I could continue even while I was pregnant.

"Can I still run?" I nervously asked my obstetrician at my first appointment, all the while scared of his response. I was worried that it might not be safe to continue to run during pregnancy.

"Yes," was his response, accompanied by some cautious, wise advice. I was already a runner so it was okay to keep doing what I had been doing; I had to make sure I didn't overheat my body, maintain my heart rate below 140 beats per minute, and listen carefully to my body.

"Awesome, this is a good thing," he added. "Maintaining your running will help you during labour. Your body will let you know when it doesn't want to run anymore."

1st Trimester

The good thing about the first trimester is that chances are you won't put on much more than 3 kilo of weight. And if you are one of the more than 60% of women who suffer from morning sickness, you might not put on any weight at all.

Therefore, if you were like me and became pregnant while training, just keep going.

Evette running when she was pregnant

Many people have asked me how I managed to work full-time, travel overseas every couple of weeks as well as maintain my running schedule while being pregnant. My secret is simple — running is an effective life tool. Running helped me through my pregnancy in many different ways.

I like to run first thing in the morning before the sun rises and the rest of the world awakens. This helps me get a head start on my day, organize my thoughts and plan for the day ahead. During my first trimester, running in the morning helped keep my nausea at bay — the queasiness in my stomach would disappear within a few minutes into the morning run. I couldn't manage to keep up the same schedule as prior to pregnancy, but I managed to run at least four times a week, while covering much shorter distances on days when I felt tired.

During my first trimester, I also struggled most with fatigue and hunger. I had become accustomed to a lingering sense of fatigue and found that my food intake was critical to keeping my energy levels up. I could not stop eating nor stop thinking about eating. Making sure you are eating enough healthy food is critical throughout your pregnancy and postpartum phase, especially if you plan to continue to run. Remember you are eating for two people! I ate as healthy as possible, and tried to have six smaller meals a day rather than three large meals. However, I also managed to fit in two to four litres of ice cream a week!

Some people like to meditate, do yoga, go for a walk, read a book or watch television to relax and unwind — I like to run. The natural highs of running kept my moods elevated and kept me chilled throughout my pregnancy. I can honestly say I have never felt so good in my life as I did when I was pregnant. The endorphins generated by running seemed to continue throughout the day.

I like to run when I travel for work. I often don't have the time on business trips to fit in any proper sightseeing, so instead I head out early in the mornings before my meetings to explore a city. In fact, my pregnant belly was taken on tour to Singapore, USA, China, Cambodia, Mexico and Japan.

2nd Trimester

I continued my sightseeing running tours on business trips well into the fifth month of my pregnancy, despite the disapproving stares I received along the way. Especially when I was pregnant, running helped me acclimatize to different time zones.

My last overseas trip was to China when I was five-and-a-half month pregnant. The work schedule was hectic and I had been working long days — I was conducting research in three different cities across China. As crazy as it seems, running during pregnancy and while travelling actually kept my energy levels up, I had much more energy on the days I ran. On my last trip I only ran in the mornings in the hotel gym; the pollution outside was too much. One morning after a run I ducked into the local Starbucks to grab a coffee. To my amusement, the staff would not serve me. I was told that I was "with child" and "coffee not good for you." I managed to convince the young girl serving me that even though I was "with child" my doctor had allowed me to drink one cup of coffee per day. I'm not sure how they would have reacted to seeing me run that morning!

Every individual and every pregnancy is different, and the best advice I can give is to listen to your body. You will need to modify your running — the intensity, frequency and speed. Put the brakes on . . . pregnancy is not a time to push yourself, you can change your running course or stop timing your runs so you don't have any benchmarks to judge yourself against. Running is to be enjoyed; if you don't enjoy it, then don't do it!

The second trimester was the most enjoyable for running. I had lost the constant fatigue of the first trimester and I felt good, amazing even! The frequency of my toilet visits increased exponentially and this meant planning my runs around toilets; although I didn't always need to stop, it was reassuring to know that I could if I needed to.

In the second trimester I only put on another 4 kilos. Running had kept my weight gain to a healthy level and seemed to also prevent fluid retention, something very common among expectant mothers.

However, my pregnancy wasn't entirely smooth sailing. In the second trimester I decided to take up yoga. I thought it would be a nice complement to my running, I would cross-train in a less energetic and low impact way, especially now that I had started to gain more weight. How wrong I was! It took only one session in which I stretched my body a little further than I should have, easily done with relaxin coursing through your body (relaxin is the hormone that turns you into a rubber woman) and I ended up with osteopubis. Osteopubis is inflammation of the pubic symphysis; the point where the left and right pubic bones meet at the front of the pelvic girdle. What that means is every time I tried to run I felt excruciating pain through my pelvis. People most at risk of osteopubis are those who participate in running events. Ironically, I had developed this condition from yoga.

Yoga itself wasn't the problem. I had started something completely new during my pregnancy. If I had been doing yoga before pregnancy, like my running, I may have prevented this condition. I was frustrated and disappointed as I was enjoying my running more than ever. For a few weeks I was forced to give up running; instead, I swam and cycled. Luckily, with some rest, a pelvic belt, physio pilates, and perseverance, I was able to get the condition under control and resume running.

Last Trimester

Several weeks into my last trimester (I was thirty weeks pregnant), I faced another obstacle. The impact of my weight gain, coupled with the troublesome hormone relaxin, was creating problems for me. I had endured lower back issues for many years — I had spondylolisthesis and a disk bulge. The physiotherapist who had treated me for more than ten years wasn't sure I was even going to run during my pregnancy. My back had flared up a few times throughout the pregnancy, so wearing a stretchy bandage like a brace around my pelvis and attending Pilates sessions at least once a week seemed to hold everything in place. At thirty-five weeks and into my third pair of runners since the start of my pregnancy, I felt ready to stop running. The baby had dropped and while I felt good enough to continue running, my body told me it was time to stop. Instead, I substituted my running with walking, which I continued right up until the day my water bag broke. On the day I went into labour, I had walked a very leisurely six kilometres. After a very long 24-hour labour, I delivered a healthy baby boy, Jasper, born 7 pounds, 6 ounces, at thirty-eight weeks.

Postpartum

Almost immediately postpartum, I was ready to continue my exercise routine. But how soon is too soon? The general rule of thumb for embarking on rigorous exercise is after the six-week postnatal check. I started walking in the hospital, albeit only a few laps of the ward. On day five when I was sent home from the hospital, I managed an easy 4-kilometre walk outside in the beautiful sunshine with the pram. I didn't resume running until my body was ready. A key part of my recovery included intensive pelvic floor exercises. I resumed running six weeks postpartum, easing into it with run-walks before running continuously.

At the end of week eight, I competed in my first fun run, a 14-kilometre "Run for the Kids" event around the streets of Melbourne. It was tough going but I felt great, and I am convinced my pregnancy gave me a significant boost. Competing so close to giving birth, I had all of that extra blood and oxygen circulating through my body, though perhaps it was more psychological, especially since I had survived childbirth, which was worse than any training session. It felt so good physically and emotionally to run across the finish line and pick up my baby boy into my arms — I felt alive!

I am not the only one who has not let pregnancy slow her down. Paula Radcliffe, the current marathon world record holder, ran throughout her pregnancy, even running on the day she gave birth to a healthy baby girl Isla, in 2007. And twelve days after Isla's birth, she started running again. Paula made her marathon return at the New York City Marathon ten months postpartum, which she won with an official time of 2:23:09. Amazing stuff!

You don't have to be an Olympic champion to continue running during your pregnancy but you do need to have been a runner before pregnancy. Always listen to your body and your doctor's advice. Consider mixing up your running during pregnancy with other less weight-bearing activities such as walking and swimming.

Key Learnings

Check with your doctors and tell them what you plan to do.

If you are already a runner, you should be able to continue running during pregnancy; everyone and every pregnancy is different so be guided by your doctor.

Don't start anything new.

Pregnancy is not a time to train or to build up your running — it is a time to maintain or reduce it.

Aim to keep your running speed conversational — you are trying too hard if you can't run and talk.

Watch out for the hormone Relaxin.

Keep well hydrated and make sure you are eating enough quality food.

Ensure you have the right shoe support — consult an expert.

Enjoy your pregnancy — it's good for both of you.

6

~

Unlearning to Learn

"It's what you learn after you know it all that counts."

– John Wooden

When I joined Nestlé after Unilever I had to unlearn several of the Unilever systems, and begin to learn the Nestlé way of doing things. So there was a process of unlearning in order to learn that was required to fit into a working, productive system, though the goals were essentially the same — understanding which consumer needs you are seeking to meet, producing, marketing, selling, and turning out profits.

Often, even within the same role, or while working on a team or in a project, you find that sometimes you have to take one step backward to move two steps forward. This, in a sense, is another way of unlearning or stepping back, albeit not quite the same.

While training for my first marathon, I realized that it was not as simple as stepping up training week and after week, culminating in a full marathon. I realized that training schedules are scientifically formulated with a lighter week following two heavier weeks of build up. The body needs a "relative rest period." You cannot be firing on all cylinders all the time, or you will burn out and lose momentum. Therefore, there was the one backward step to be taken for every two steps forward, and I found that over the course of the 18-week training I was ready for the gruelling 42.195 kilometres (26.2 miles) distance. The one step back was critical. This was another type of unlearning.

The journal that I kept during my training runs, was also of great value. At the end of each run I wrote down how I felt physically and psychologically, and then noted if I had slept well or long enough the night before, the terrain I was running on, whether it was windy, cool or humid. Analysing bad days brought up good insights and learnings. If we stop learning from unsuccessful experiences, we start looking towards a downward spiral and an ecosystem of failure.

> "Every failure brings with it the seed of an equivalent success." – Napoleon Hill

A third, and more basic, level of unlearning in order to learn is when having learnt on your own, and reached a certain stage, you then plan to take a quantum leap. Often we realize that what is required is not harder work, but a smarter way of doing the same thing. For instance, in sports it is about technique and style perfection — to achieve twice of what you could do earlier, but with less than twice the effort. This is somewhat akin to what you encounter while rising up the corporate ladder. Teamwork, leadership, dealing with complexity and energy become more important. These are the skills that need to be honed more and more, while technical expertise becomes relatively less important.

> You need to learn that what got you here is not going to get you there.

This is exactly what I had to learn the hard way during training for my first marathon — the 2001 Chicago Marathon.

Shoe Learnings

When I walked into the runners shoe store in Barrington, Illinois, ten miles away from my home, I was clear about what I needed to buy — a pair of running shoes.

"So do you need motion control shoes or cushioned shoes?" asked the friendly young sales rep whom I later realized was also a runner, which was a pre-requisite to be a sales rep at that store. I wondered what language he was speaking. I told him I was preparing to run my first marathon. After congratulating me heartily on my decision to run the Chicago Marathon, he asked me if any specific brand worked better for me, at which point I balked again. He was gone for a few minutes and came back with four pairs of shoes: Asics, Mizuno, New Balance and Brooks. I had never heard of any of these brands, and was a bit concerned as they were all mostly white and close to US $90 each.

"Don't you have any Reebok or Nike?" I asked.

"We keep running shoes, not party shoes," was his reply with a smile; I presume he was amused by my question. He asked me to try out the shoes and see which suited me better. At this point I finally laughed and told him that I had no clue what to look for because thus far I had bought my shoes on the basis of price and colour. Then I opened my ears and started listening to him.

Shoes had to be bought not based on colour, design and price as I had done until now, but on technical functionality, to match my feet's requirement:

- Did I overpronate or supinate?
- Were both my feet and legs symmetrical?
- Did I have any other peculiarity that needed to be compensated for by my shoes?
- Was I basically a treadmill runner?
- Did I run on trails and uneven surfaces?
- Did I run mainly on mud and clay or on tar and concrete?
- How much and how often was I running?
- Was I predominantly a heel striker?

I was in a new world learning a lot of new things in my forty-first year, and unlearning just as many things with which I had grown up.

While buying my running shoes I realized that they needed to be a size bigger than my regular shoes, because feet swell while running long distance. I also needed to go shopping in the afternoon with the socks I would generally wear, rather than in the morning; again because feet tend to swell a bit over the course of the day. Back in India, the shoe sales reps would always tell me that my work shoes would loosen up over time so I needed to buy them snug; but now for running shoes I had to buy them loose so that they would get snug during the run.

Gear Learnings

I was a happy purchaser at the end of that long shopping session and walked out of the store with a pair of New Balance 854 shoes. I was also happy that I had not been suckered into buying running T-shirts, shorts, undergarments and socks. I had pure cotton ones and did not need a slick sales rep to sell me any more of his "fancy" running gear.

I was soon to unlearn my faith in pure cotton.

After my first 18-miler I had: blistered feet with the cotton towel socks soaked and wrinkled, nipples sore as hell but luckily not bleeding yet, and a chafed groin due to my inner wear. This was the quickest lesson in unlearning in order to learn. I went back to Barrington the next day and spent a couple of hours in the sports store. I had to invest in shorts, T-shirts, undergarments, socks and a headband — all synthetic and made of wicking fabric that made sure I remained dry while the sweat evaporated fast and cooled my body over the distance. I learnt that there are no absolutes, and that things change with time, new technology, research and new learnings. It is critical to have an open mind, else we can remain in a rut shaped by the past and move forward much slower than we could otherwise. Unlearning is a critical part of continuous learning.

On my first ever long weekend run of fourteen miles I had learnt about the value of a water bottle as I dodged in and out of McDonald's outlets and restaurants and sweated in the sun. I always carry a water bottle with me since that run, no matter how short the run.

Training Learnings

After this run, I also realized that there was nothing that was impossible: tough — yes, not done before — yes, but impossible — no! This learning has carried me through many rough situations while training for long distance running as well as at work. It's all in the mind to a large extent, and if you put your mind to it and start working on smarter ways of doing things, collaborating, asking others for advice, and so on, the seemingly impossible things become do-able. Thus, as you step up from a 5-kilometre race to a 10-kilometre race to a half-marathon to a full marathon, you find the challenges of technique, form, gear, schedules and nutrition gaining more and more importance.

Speed and Distance Learnings

Marathon training was not just focused on going longer and longer distances. Much more was required:

- Strength had to be built in the gym;
- Speed had to be increased *via* structured interval training and hill training;
- Flexibility was required *via* still and dynamic stretching and yoga;
- Sleep and rest were gaining more importance — not just hours of sleep but sleep quality — and there was a need to de-stress;
- Hydration and nutrition began to play a more important role. I became much more aware of what, when and how much I was eating and drinking;
- And, finally, the focus shifted to building mental toughness and psychological optimism by breaking down various barriers one by one, and by setting an audacious goal to keep the motivation and discipline going.

However, the biggest lesson that I have learnt is that you still have to listen to your body. You cannot be pig-headed and stubborn, else you will be on a sure route to a medical emergency.

In 2008, I put together a 7-week training schedule that has been used by thousands of runners since to aid them in improving both speed and stamina while running.

This is reproduced as Table 6.1. Try this simple 7-week plan to improve your stamina, pace and VO2 MAX (which simply put is one measure of fitness of a runner and measures the maximum volume of oxygen the athlete can use per unit of body weight, per minute, at your peak performance).

Table 6.1

7-Week Training Schedule for Improving Speed and Stamina

Wk	Monday	Tuesday	Wednesday	Thursday	Friday	Saturday	Sunday
1.	30 - 45 mins cross train	Run / Walk 5 km	3 repeats 400 m	Tempo run 30 mins	Rest	4 km medium pace	Long slow run 6 km
2.	30 - 45 mins cross train	Run / Walk 5 km	4 repeats 400 m	Tempo run 40 mins	Rest	4 km medium pace	Long slow run 7 km
3.	30 - 45 mins cross train	Run / Walk 5 km	5 repeats 400 m	Tempo run 45 mins	Rest	5 km medium pace	Long slow run 8 km

Contd . . .

Table 6.1 *(. . . contd)*

Wk	Monday	Tuesday	Wednesday	Thursday	Friday	Saturday	Sunday
4.	30 - 45 mins cross train	Run / Walk 5 km	4 repeats 400 m	Tempo run 40 mins	Rest	4 km medium pace	Long slow run 7 km
5.	30 - 45 mins cross train	Run / Walk 5 km	5 repeats 400 m	Tempo run 45 mins	Rest	4 km medium pace	Long slow run 8 km
6.	30 - 45 mins cross train	Run / Walk 5 km	6 repeats 400 m	Tempo run 50 mins	Rest	4 km medium pace	Long slow run 9 km
7.	30 - 45 mins cross train	Run / Walk 5 km	4 repeats 400 m	Tempo run 30 mins	Rest	6 km medium pace	Long slow run 10 km

Notes:

Cross Train: Some cardio exercise other than running, it could be cycling, swimming, paying tennis, etc.

400 m repeats: Warm up with 10 to 15 minutes of running, run 400 metre at your race pace for a 1 kilometre race, cool down and get your breathing and heart rate back to normal, and then repeat the cycle again. Finally, cool down with a 10 to 15 minute run and stretch.

Tempo run 30 minutes: Run for 5 minutes at a pace slower than your 10-kilometre race pace to warm up. Run the next 5 minutes at your 10-kilometre race pace as you ramp up. Next 5 minutes at 5-kilometre race pace. Mid 5 minutes at your 1-kilometre race pace. And then reverse the sequence as you slow down.

Medium pace: Run at your 10-kilometre race pace.

Long slow run: Run 20 sec/km slower than your 10-kilometre race pace.

Conditions and Learnings: Weather/Altitude/Terrain

My 42nd marathon up in the Himalaya was my first attempt at running at an altitude of 11,000 feet. Friends thought that this would be a piece of cake for me. I was, however, quite nervous, as I had never run at such an altitude before. I had been on mountaineering trips that were at significantly higher altitudes, but that was thirty years earlier. How would my body take it now, especially the lungs? How could I sensibly acclimatize to the altitude and also make sure I had fun, since I was also going to be a photographer and a race director? These and several other questions and concerns raced through my head. I had to learn fast. Else, a long run can humble you and bring you down automatically!

The view during the run was gorgeous but I focused on the job at hand as a race director — I had to look into the safety aspects, the fun aspects, photograph participants, as well as the breathtakingly scenic vistas, stay in telephonic touch with the medical team and other volunteers, and weave my own participation into the race.

As it happened I had an exceedingly memorable run through perhaps the most scenic route I had ever been on. Running a marathon is not always about the best timing but this one was focused on having the best time. Beaming smiles at the finish line were more important than my own finish time.

No matter how much and how well you train, even mimicking as much of the conditions of the location you are going to be running in, nothing beats acclimatization at the real location. Most of us get focused if the run is at a high altitude but this rule applies even when you are going to a warm place from a cool one, or going to run in a place that is significantly more humid than where you have been training, or if the terrain is cross country or has significant ups and downs.

Training for a new environment while you remain in your current environ requires a lot of adaptation and unlearning along the way.

360-Degree Training

To build up stamina and speed, your heart and lungs need to be exercised with tempo runs and repeats, your flexibility and strength need to be enhanced in addition to your running workouts, some cross training is needed for an all-body exercise and relaxation of running specific muscles, and nutrition and hydration need to be focused on. All-in-all, a 360-degree approach is required — there is no single magic bullet.

It's not just running in your training program that will improve your performance. You also need to include various aspects of your lifestyle — sleeping, eating habits, quality, quantity and timing of intake, flexibility, muscle strengthening and other cardiovascular activities for all-round health, monitoring health metrics to see that you are being sensible in your training, and so much more. It would even include the friends you make while running. Your focus has to be sharp for realizing the most out of what you are putting in.

I have found that running has made me unconsciously alter many aspects of my lifestyle:

- I started going to bed earlier and also getting up fifteen minutes earlier each morning, until I was sleeping all of an hour earlier than before.
- I'm not the last person at the bar any longer. At a party, I drink more water and fresh juice, and eat more salads and raw veggies and less red meat.
- I focus on stretching, and my flexibility has improved bit by tiny bit. I also started going to the gym once a week during training to focus on strengthening a few muscles.
- I started getting more disciplined about my time in general, and also taking rest seriously.

Running has truly had a 360-degree impact on my life from the inside out; and in all ways it has worked for the better. Try it for yourself.

Unlearn and Learn

I guess the unspoken unlearning and learning that we go through when we get married is all about being open to another point of view, and about realizing how we are often stuck in our ways. I would say a 100-kilometre ultramarathon over a few days would be the best honeymoon — keep everyone humble and open to suggestions on how to take things forward, painlessly. Then again, if you get a different boss at the same job that you have done for a while, and you are required to think and do differently, it's a different learning and unlearning that happens.

Running, and especially long distance running, opens you up to new approaches, while being humbled if you do not.

There's No Such Thing as Failure

I am a true believer that there is no such thing as failure — failure is only the lack of appropriate learning and effort.

Unlearn as things change, as new information comes up, and as new technologies are introduced. Seek to constantly soak in and learn.

Every experience is a potential learning experience.

Keep learning why a changing environment makes the same task different — why a hilly 5-kilometre run differs from a flat one at sea level, or from a flat 5-kilometre run in Tibet, or in the Sahara, or in the Antarctic.

Re-examine the assumptions you grew up with.

Review your dream: Is it based on yesterday's learning, or the unlearning of today and the learning of tomorrow?

Experience the new, and move on, forward.

And that's when commitment needs to kick in, and work with a 360-degree approach.

Running and Living

Great managers are multifaceted and are good with people, apart from being sharp, strategic, tactical, operational, comfortable with varied subject matter and . . . but above all, keen learners, which also meant that they have to be able to unlearn and re-learn, when required. The more I run and read about the science of running, the more parallels I find it has with life —and staying on top of the game, injury free.

~

7

~

Commitment and Focus

"The minute you start talking about what you're going to do if you lose, you have lost."

– George Shultz

I was at the 5-mile mark in my second marathon, also in Chicago, on a cool October morning in 2002. I was near Lincoln Park when I started to feel some pain in my right knee. I had 21.2 miles still to go and a part of me began thinking the worst, "I can't walk 21 miles and finish in time, nor do I want to run and injure my knee," and various other thoughts that became more and more negative. "Should I stop and opt out or should I carry on?" I was limping a bit now and with the limp the ache was less. I decided to continue for another mile and get it checked at the next medical post. Then I began to focus on what a great day it was — clear blue skies, thousands of runners — and also on the reason I was there. I was running to have fun and not agonize about an ache. I had run this distance many times. I had already run more than five miles of the marathon and I was committed to finishing it, even if the timing was not going to be great. Surprisingly, by around the 7-mile mark, the ache and pain were gone and I was running as if nothing had ever happened. I was also getting back on track to achieve my goal of running at a pace of nine minutes per mile; or in other words finishing the run within 3 hours and 56 minutes.

Ultimately I was a very proud finisher at 3 hours and 51 minutes, which was a good 41 minutes faster than my first marathon. At the time, I didn't quite know how this happened. In hindsight, I put it down to a continued focus on the positives, good training, the fact that I had run a full marathon earlier, that I was already past the 5-mile mark when I felt the knee pain, and that I had been doing a better pace this time around. In sum, cutting out negative thoughts about what would happen if I had to drop out, how I would feel, etc., was a bit easier to manage. Most of all it was my commitment to make it to the finish line with a smile that helped.

No matter how daunting the obstacles, how slim the chances of achieving the goal, the important thing is to stay committed and focused on the task at hand. This was all the more obvious to me during my second marathon as I've described above, because somehow the commitment made light of all the negatives, and when the positive thoughts kicked in, I was on a roll.

That incident has helped me over the years, whenever I felt that the task at hand seemed daunting and the chips seemed stacked against success.

Notwithstanding my punishing work schedule, with a lot of long distance travel thrown in at that time, I stayed wedded to my running schedule. It gave me the discipline to carry on despite the odds — rain, heat, and fatigue. The habit also honed my ability to stay focused on the goal at hand rather than the obstacles along the way. But it needed loads of commitment and focus! I would often find myself staying relentlessly committed to the schedule. Solutions, rather than problems, became the focus of all my attention. At times, I have run to a friend's house to attend a dinner party to put in my training. Setting a goal, a good training plan followed with discipline, keeping track of the metrics of progress and smaller sub-goals to recalibrate the journey, and celebrating the smaller wins along the way — these were the key. No rocket science this . . . all these are things that we learn over the years, but perhaps forget to practise with rigour.

Big Dreams, Small Steps

In July 2007 I was running my second San Francisco Marathon and had slipped in my pursuit of the goal I had set out — to finish in four hours. I had crossed the half-way point. Coming down Haight Street and picking up speed, smiling and waving to the spectators, taking pictures with my trusted

Running and Living

Some questions I often get asked are:

Are you using running to illustrate how to reach milestones and goals in life, or are you imparting information and your experience to merely make me a better runner?

And here the answer is categorically the former. This is not the definitive book to make you a better runner. It may perhaps get you to think about starting to run if you are not currently doing so, or push you into challenging yourself beyond what you are doing currently.

Does one become a better person or a better decision-maker as a result of becoming a runner, or is running a means to get a "high" regardless of what may be happening to the rest of one's life?

Numerous studies, testimonials and more have shown that running makes you fitter, healthier, more humble, more open, more patient, and then more self confident and optimistic — and you begin to feel anything is possible. Apart from that you get more energized, with a sharper memory, have lower stress levels than if you were not running. The runner's high gives you a feel-good to last you through many tough situations while still feeling good and on a "high." This is not a dream, it is real! I would go on to stick my neck out and state — running can make you into a better person, a better leader, a better risk taker, and more.

So this book is not all about running. It is about you and life. And it's about how running is an addictive tool to learn from.

waterproof digital camera, I suddenly felt a shooting pain in my right shin.

Shin splint, stress fracture, or something else? I wasn't sure as I started hobbling on my approach to the Bay Front. Perhaps my lack of downhill training, coupled with my enthusiasm to make up time had got the better of me. Now the revised goal of 4 hours and 30 minutes was also looking out of reach and maybe a finish was not going to happen. The thought of a "Did not finish" mark against my name, after having come all the way from India for this run after a fall on my back at home while trying to change a light bulb, got to me. I walked slowly for another 500 metres, and then said to myself, "I am going to overtake 50 finishers before I reach the finish line and then I am going to sprint the last 100 metres." That focus got me to think of the positives, the goal at hand and my commitment to achieve this new goal. I started off at a reasonable clip along the bay, passing the Giants' stadium and the Port area. Soon, I found I had passed 35 people, but with still half a mile to go, I was out of breath, so I took a walking break and five people passed me by. Surprisingly there was no shin pain any more and I took off again. Well, "took off" is probably not the right phrase because it is Ussain Bolt who takes off; however for me, it *was* like taking off. I was counting again as I passed other runners and the number climbed back up to 35, and reached 40. I could see the finish line ahead of me and not too many runners ahead — could I overtake them and make it to 50? With 400 metres to go, I started sprinting. Would I be able to hold out for 400 metres as I had planned to sprint only the last 100 metres? I passed 43, 44, then 45 runners, and then my pace actually increased. I was no longer taking pictures but was focused on the six runners between me and the finish line. Runner numbers 46, 47, and then I ran faster than I have ever run in any marathon and crossed the finish line as I overtook number 49. But I had a smile on my face. I was ecstatic! I had finished another marathon, and even though my goals had been revised a few times during the run, I was glad that I had managed to do what I did in the last mile and end on a high!

Breaking things down into bite-sized chunks, like overtaking 50 runners, going past that runner just ahead of you, and so on, made each mini-goal measurable and the small win motivational. Again, here was something I realized in hindsight, and yet another basic life lesson was reiterated to me *via* running.

> Focus and commitment had helped me be a winner for myself. No one else would ever understand, and I was not going to crow about this to anyone else in any case.

Four hours and 32 minutes is not a fast time, in fact it was exactly the same time as that of my first marathon, but I had won the race for myself *versus* my mind, and had beaten that little guy who was pounding my brain, saying "Are you crazy? Why are you doing this? Stop. Give up. See a doctor."

Running and Living

Whenever I went off track at work or felt that something was insurmountable, I would think back to one of my long runs or marathons in which I had come out on top despite the odds, and that would give me a positive surge of energy. I was already committed to the job at hand, so how could I ever leave it half done? Then again, running helped me cut out the distractions outside the job and remain focused, while enabling me to appreciate the enjoyable things along the way, and sometimes create some fun of my own.

Celebrate Each Win, Smile Along the Way

At around the 35-kilometre mark in the 56-kilometre 2 Oceans Marathon in Cape Town, South Africa, in 2009, I was tired. The steady climb up Chapman's Peak was breath-takingly beautiful, the view across Hout Bay was awesome, but I found that the gradient had also taken my breath away. As I walked and jogged upwards I found many others doing the same. I ran up to Moses, a fellow runner, and asked him to "part the waters" so that we could cut out some miles from the route. Then I turned to Justice, another South African runner that no matter what happened to the rest of us, he must power on hard: "Because Justice delayed would be justice denied!" Both responded with shouts of laughter, and so the humour kept my mind off the toil ahead. We chattered through the next five miles and forgot about our pain along the way.

Working with our Global Market Research Partner TNS, we would end our six-monthly gigantic analyses and presentation sessions across the corporation with a fun team dinner with the most absurd "gifts." A good laugh kept us focused but also in good humour and hopefully more committed to the tasks at hand . . . distance running had taught me many more things than I had ever dreamt of.

Commitment and focus were now part of my lexicon. Nothing really seemed insurmountable. No obstacle on the way was ever the focus; the focus was on getting around the obstacle or tackling the problem.

~

We all get challenged at various times in our work or personal life, and sometimes that focus makes us sharper and clearer and makes us stand out. It's the commitment that sees us through tougher times. I have learnt much from running, especially long distance running, about sharpening that commitment and focus.

Try training for a distance greater than what you have run so far, and it will enhance your appreciation of what commitment and focus will do for you.

~

8

~

Humility Revisited

The Fine Line between Self Confidence and Arrogance

"You also need to look back, not just at the people who are running behind you but especially at those who don't run and never will . . . those who run but don't race . . . those who started training for a race but didn't carry through . . . those who got to the starting line but didn't reach the finish line . . . those who once raced better than you but no longer run at all. You're still here. Take pride in wherever you finish. Look at all the people you've outlasted."

– Joe Henderson

What Joe Henderson says is so true!

It also sounds straight out of a business book.

How many firms that featured in the US Fortune 100 in 1999 had dropped out of the list by 2009?

Any guesses? 39!

Bought, went bust, slipped-up or just plain disappeared. These included #13 Mobil (bought by Exxon), #19 Merrill Lynch, #21 Kmart Holdings, and #27, the infamous Enron.

Success very often breeds complacency, inflated ego, pure sluggishness, and, in the worst case, greed and dishonesty. As in business, so also in running. There is Enron and likewise there are doping athletes. There are athletes who made it big in one race and faded away, and there are companies that did phenomenally well with one product, like Motorola with the RAZR phone, and then just slid away and disappeared. Humility is the one characteristic that would have helped the decision makers in these corporations.

Then, too, perhaps long distance running also may be a good way to learn the lesson of humility and personal introspection.

I have been humbled many a time when I did not train adequately for a marathon but felt overconfident that I could finish comfortably in the four-hour time frame, but did not. I did not put in the required effort, and I did not get the required result. So what if I had done a quicker marathon on many occasions earlier? That did not matter. It was much like Wall Street. What have you achieved in the last quarter?

> "I'm often credited with the motto, 'Only the paranoid survive.' When it comes to business, I believe in the value of paranoia. Business success contains the seeds of its own destruction. The more successful you are, the more people want a chunk of your business, and then another chunk, and then another until there is nothing left." – Andy Grove

"I don't need a schedule any longer . . ."

"I will continue to run faster and longer . . ."

"I know all I need to know about running . . ."

"I have never been injured . . ."

I hear all this very often, especially from people who have been running for about a year or two. However, I believe that we should never stop listening to our bodies. We get a bit older with each season and there are new learnings with each passing year. The most important thing is to be absolutely aware of the issues and to listen to your body, or else there will be a big one coming up. And presto! These same people have been humbled by a severe hamstring pull, or an iliotibial band injury, or just sheer fatigue reducing their performance. I had a hamstring pull during an ultra race a few months after my 89-kilometre Comrades run, and had to pull out around the 40-kilometre mark. I had to use the ambulance for the first time in my life and added a "Did not finish" to my running CV.

There are always newer and better — or perhaps older and better — ways to do things. If you haven't planned well, not strategized and, most importantly, not executed, you are going to be humbled, or perhaps injured.

The most critical thing in life — and in running — is to be humble or you will be humbled.

Running and reading also have parallels. To continue with Will Smith's *Key to Life,* where he describes why reading is important, and goes on to say that a gazillion people in this world have faced every situation that you may possibly face and have written about it. So when you read, you might well find a solution that helps you move on. That's the equivalent of keeping an open mind, listening and reading constantly; to become your own best coach.

Take running for example — if you are a regular marathoner and run two to three marathons a year evenly spaced out and take a three-month break from running, you need to resume your training on the ground floor of the training schedule. Do not try to start from where you left off, even if you have been an active cyclist or swimmer during the gap period. Each sport uses different muscles and needs a different focus. Also, life is full of inflexion points where neither is the past a predictor of the future and nor do regular patterns experienced by others necessarily come to pass for you.

The most important thing about being human is our ability to analyse what has happened, get to the root cause, and change course or fix the issue. But every so often we get pig-headed, complacent or lazy, as happened to me in November 2009 when I was running my longest run then — 75 kilometres. I had run 29 marathons by then and took my training lightly and barely did any long runs. I did not train long enough in the shoes that I was going to run in, and had not done a long run with the two extra insoles in my right shoe; I had discovered before my Two Oceans Run, earlier in May, that one of my legs was effectively shorter than the other because of the way I ran. All these are basics for a long distance run and a cardinal sin for one to ignore them and take them lightly. I paid the price.

A Few Learnings for Life After a 75-Kilometre Run

I ran a 75-kilometre run in Bangalore and am listing out a few simple home truths that came up to the fore ever so sharply, all over again.

To Run Long, You Must Train Long

I had not trained appropriately, and five days prior to the run I had banged my left knee badly on a banister at home. Till the final morning I was in two minds about whether I should run or not. And then I decided to get to the start line and see how it went — kilometre after kilometre. I had not run long enough in training and paid the price, being humbled and forced to walk far more than I had planned to. I find the same applies to anything in life; there are no short cuts for achieving a big goal.

Cheering is Key: When You Cheer Others, Others Start Cheering You

The only good thing I did while running was to stop after two loops, i.e. every 25 kilometres, pick up my guitar which I had left at the start point, belt out a song or two, unwind, and carry on. I cheered each runner as he or she passed me and, after some time, I heard and saw many more cheers for me, which kept me going. Closer to the finish when we were very tired, a thumbs-up sign or a smile would do it. Smiling helps de-stress — it is a simple tool we have been blessed with but one we don't use adequately. We mistakenly think that the world will collapse if we don't remain absolutely serious about life!

Humility Revisited

Blistered, aching and exhausted, I contemplated giving up on several occasions. I had been humbled, and had learnt a lesson. It's good to revisit humility once in a while.

Start a running program, keep a training log and learn from your good days and bad days, stretch yourself, do your personal best, get on a high, and stay injury free. And if your performance dips or you get injured, listen to your body, consult a doctor of sports medicine, listen to other runners, review your schedule, and remember that you are human.

Long distance running is like business. Training in the last quarter is what is important; history is history, which the mind and body soon forget.

No Problem is So Large That It is Insurmountable

Almost a year later in March 2010, on 8 March to be precise, I began training for the 89-kilometre Comrades Ultra Marathon in South Africa, from Pietermaritzburg to Durban. I had started my training in right earnest, albeit belatedly. I had learnt from experience in my 75-kilometre run and did not want to repeat the same mistakes — that would be stupidity. So I plunged into some weight training, flexibility schedules, long distance and hill running to get prepared for both the ups and the downs that the Comrades Marathon included. The downs take a huge toll on the quads, knees and the muscles, and my body would need training to be able to take that pounding, or I would have a "Did not finish," against my name. So back to focus and commitment, getting over starting pains, focusing on humility and not resting on past laurels, yet keeping them in view for motivation — all that and more was going to be required now.

March 14, 2010, 8 p.m.: I survived a crucial 34-kilometre run and was elated. My confidence had started growing. I was aching a bit because it had been a sharp increase in distance, but the run seemed to fly by even though I went slowly, and took several walking breaks. A running buddy, Randeep, joined me. His longest run before this was 25 kilometres, but on this day he did 35 kilometres. He had been a real hero and kept me motivated, as we chatted about running, our kids' interests, marital discord resulting from running, and much more. This was an up and down course, chosen because it had a few "hills", so that I could practise the ups and downs I would encounter prior to entering Durban.

March 21, 2010: I started the run at 4 a.m. when it was pitch dark, with dogs barking at various locations. There was some truck traffic and a car with two drunks. "You bloody joggers!" one of them shouted. Randeep and I were glad they were drunk and would have difficulty turning their car around, so we didn't respond and just continued running and chatting. I managed 42 kilometres that day, ran 11 kilometres slowly the next day, and another 12 kilometres the day after. I rested on Wednesday as I drove to Chandigarh and then Shimla, to get some ground work done for our ensuing runs in April and October, respectively. A reconnaissance run to toughen our planned second Shimla Half Marathon had me doing a difficult hilly run of 26 kilometres on Thursday. This was followed by a half marathon, mainly downhill from Shimla. My driver picked me up a few hours later. The next morning six of us ran, starting off at 4:30 a.m. in the dark, and discovered a lovely trail in the Aravalli hills; parts of that route has now become our infamously tough Town and Country Cross Country Half Marathon. I managed to complete 32 kilometres. The dogs had stopped barking because they knew it was perhaps the same crazy bunch of humans running past again. So I ended that week with 140 kilometres of running. The most I had ever done before was 80 kilometres so this was a huge milestone for me, as well as a great confidence booster. I now felt confident about completing an 89-kilometre hill run without major incident, but had to work on my pace to make sure I finished within the maximum time limit of 12 hours. I had a long way to go in training for that, and there was no room for complacency. Humility revisited yet again!

May 30, 2010, D Day: I was in Pietermaritzburg at 5 a.m. at the start of the Comrades Marathon — nervous, excited yet strangely relaxed. Several people had wished me luck, and I knew I had to be sensible during the run. A few South African runners whom I had met the previous day and even during the run gave loads of advice, but the one common thing they all said was: "Give the Comrades respect, and you'll do fine!"

Armed with my camera I was clicking photographs and videos as we went along, having a blast as I went out at a pace slightly more conservative than planned. There were five hills — Polly Shorts, Inchanga, Bothas, Fields and Cowies. Karan, a South African who was running this gruelling distance for the fifteenth time, had pointed them out to me as he had driven us up two days before the run. But there must have been at least another forty ups and downs, which in my book would have qualified as hills. So I took them walking up and then jogging down slowly with short quick steps. Twenty-five kilometres came and went with me still running in a sea of humanity. Of the 23,000 who registered, there were around 16,000 of us who had started. I reached the half-way mark of 44.5 kilometres at Drummond in 5 hours and 45 minutes, leaving 6 hours and 15 minutes to do the latter half. The downhill slopes started when there were around 35 kilometres left to go, and this is where I got "into the zone" and started surprising myself. I felt great but did not want to push because you never know if downhill running at this stage, with fatigue, would lead to cramping or anything else. Yes, I had done a 56-kilometre training run from Shimla to Solan, which is mostly downhill, but this was different. I had to be humble and resist the temptation to speed up. At 87 kilometres, I saw two runners being carried off in ambulances — so near and yet so far. I started upping my pace just past the 87-kilometre mark and ran at a good pace when I entered the stadium, and sprinted and danced from there to the finish line. Humility had brought me to the finish line. Could I have gone faster? Perhaps. Could I have got injured? Perhaps.

~

9

~

Thinking and Doing Big

Believe that you can run farther or faster. Believe that you're young enough, old enough, strong enough, and so on to accomplish everything you want to do. Don't let worn out beliefs stop you from moving beyond yourself.

– John Bingham, *Runner's World*

What Bingham says is not just about running. It's about the life we are living.

We all encounter the "big one" — that one huge challenge in life, many a time. And that is often what makes life interesting. It is like climbing up to the top of a hill and then cutting across to the other side, to enjoy a different view.

"What am I doing here? I think I should stop!"

"I just hurt my knee at home a few days ago, that's a good enough reason to stop. Everyone knows that!"

This is the "cautious" part of your brain that talks to you when you are attempting to do something you thought was hitherto not possible.

> "Some of the world's greatest feats were accomplished by people not smart enough to know they were impossible."– Doug Larson

One such moment was during my attempt at a 75-kilometre ultra marathon in Bangalore in November 2009. That was a lot for me — my longest run prior to this was the 56-kilometre run in Cape Town that April. Yet, this was definitely not going to be my longest — I had signed up for the Comrades Marathon in South Africa, an 89-kilometre mother of ultra marathons in May 2010. After that I planned to do a 100-kilometre run in November 2010 — basically two kilometres for every year of my life because I would turn 50 by then.

The Bangalore 75-kilometre route involved 12.5-kilometre loops of an up and down course. There were runners who were doing shorter distances and, amazingly, there were some who had signed up to run 100 kilometres that day! All of them, regardless of the actual distance they were running, had signed up for something longer than what they had ever done before.

Now my friends and family know I am crazy. I had not told them much about my plans to run the Bangalore 75-kilometre because there would be inevitable rounds of advice and caution, especially from my wife and my mother, and of course, questions such as:

"Why on earth do you want to do this?"

"Isn't it too much?"

"Are you mad?"

My earlier answers to friends consisted of, "Because it is there," "I'm not sure actually," or "I want to get mentally ready to do a 100-kilometre run after turning 50."

All of these reasons were still true, but they would only cause more worry. So I told my dad two days prior to the event that I was running an ultra marathon. When he asked how much that was, I told him it was just a little more than a marathon. So, we were both relieved!

The trail was dark. All of us had flashlights and a huge cheer went up as 26 of us set out at 5 a.m., on the outskirts of a small town 30 kilometres outside Bangalore. The cloud cover made it extremely dark so all plans of running at our own respective pace from the start went for a toss as we tried to stay bunched together to avoid getting lost in the dark. This was definitely something that had never crossed my mind. One is normally supposed to run a bit slower than the target pace at the start of a long run. The best laid of plans also often need a backup plan. However, it was too beautiful, too much fun and too early to think of a Plan B, though I knew I would have to soon enough. Uneven patches, ups and downs, tree trunks in parts and a few puddles were all negotiated, while some of the chatter continued. We crossed first one water point and then another in an open meadow with no habitation in sight. Close to the end of the first loop, we "ran into" a few hundred runners who had just started their 50, 37.5, and 25 kilometre runs. That perked us up and we cheered, smiled and waved at one another.

Many people ask, "Doesn't that tire you out — all the clapping and cheering. Why expend so much energy unnecessarily?" The truth is, smiling helps you relax, and you need a lot of that in a long run when various muscles can start getting taut and tense — your neck, back and shoulders, for instance; muscles you would not necessarily think would get strained during a run. So cheering others helps cheer yourself up, and you may get a bonus payoff if someone else cheers you, too. We all need a lot of that in life; we need to relax, smile, cheer others on, and definitely, cheer ourselves on — after all we are our own most passionate cheering squad!

It was good to finish the first loop of 12.5 kilometres just as the first rays of dawn streaked across the sky. We dropped off our flashlights at the aid station, and started for the next loop. Negotiating the trail now was easy and the beauty of the surroundings seeped in. There were trees on one side and a huge meadow on the other, as we coursed around it and back into some trees, then a narrow trail through some scrub, onto a road for a kilometre, and then back to the trail for another kilometre through a forested section, and then back. I started my walking breaks as I realized I was running way beyond my targeted pace, and would have to pay the price sooner rather than later.

This time the negative thoughts started around the 30-kilometre mark. My left sole had developed a blister and a terrible ache, so I thought of stopping at the next medical aid station to get it looked at. Could I cop out at this stage? Yes, we are all human, after all. But I didn't want to give up so easily, not without a fight. I could walk more and run less and at least complete 42.2 kilometres. That would make it my 30th marathon in my life's quest to finish 50. If I was cheering everyone else, how could I stop at this stage?

I managed to run/walk to the next medical aid station. The doctor tended to my foot, put on a bandage and sent me off. I was worrying about what that would do to me, because I had a long way to go. I was only at the 35-kilometre mark and still had another 40 kilometres to cover. It felt uncomfortable, but by the time I came near the end of the loop and heard the music, a kilometre away, the left sole miraculously was pain-free, and I completed 37.5 kilometres.

I was relieved when I had the 42-kilometre mark behind me — this was my 30th marathon in eight years. And I said to myself, "It's a short distance to the 45-kilometre mark. I've done that before on the Great Ocean Road in Australia, a spectacular ultra marathon," and then once that was done, it was only 5 kilometres to the end of the loop. That's when I took a song break . . . I had brought my guitar along and had kept it at the start point. So I stopped, pulled up my guitar and belted out a song with my new running friends. That felt good. I knew this would keep me going for the next loop.

Now it was only six kilometres to the 56-kilometre mark, which I had run in Cape Town just six months before, after that it was only another 6.5 kilometres to the end of the loop at the 62.5 kilometres — and then it was just the last loop. Piece of cake! "God, what I would do for a piece of cake right now!"

My mind began to wander. I was thinking about many things . . . the flight to Singapore later that night, a dear friend's surprise 50th birthday party, figuring out the contents of this chapter, and so on.

> I find countless similarities between distance running and life, which I see as an ultra marathon.

Eleven hours after I had started running, I was on the home stretch. I had smiled at, waved at and cheered on my fellow 75-kilometre and 100-kilometre runners many times over because I understood what many were going through . . . all those running shorter distances had already finished and left. There was too much going on in my mind to feel tired or to walk, now that the end was in sight. I was running faster than I had run earlier in the day. I finished with a cheer and with a broad grin on my face. I know it may sound crazy to you. It sounds crazy to me too, in hindsight, as I write this.

Everyone cheers at the start when we are born, but then more often than not, the cheering squad thins, we pick up our own cheerleaders, plod along through uncharted teens and early work years, then marriage, kids, then adolescent kids, then retirement, and so on. Each of these was like one of my 12.5-kilometre loops — challenging, rewarding, with huge problems at times when you feel like you can't go on. These challenges need to be broken down into smaller, more manageable chunks, and that's when you get a second wind. Nothing is impossible when we break down things, think of a Plan B and a Plan C, and just keep executing. No sense in stopping and waiting for the "best plan." You need to constantly complete each chunk and keep moving forward.

You should never opt out of any loop along the course of life. Of course, things are going to be rough. And maybe that's the case for many loops in life — often consecutive ones. But focus on yourself and you'll be surprised at how much inner strength you possess. That self-talk will boost your self-confidence.

It's important to celebrate each little win, especially when times are tough, because that gives us the renewed energy to carry on stronger and to focus on positives. Many little wins make a big one. Remember, the long term comprises of many short terms, and tiny drops of water make the mighty ocean. Think of the sweat you have expended, the good times you have had, and the celebration planned at the "finish" line.

Life needs to be enjoyed and lived to the fullest. You need to be smiling at the finish line, or else what's the point? The medal and certificate is only one more reason to keep you smiling and, to me, the end-point is all about happiness.

> Erase the word "impossible" from your vocabulary and replace it with "tough."

These are some of the things that running has helped me re-examine. I now challenge myself when faced with a difficult situation, and look for ways to get to the finish line rather than continuously ponder the enormity of the problem.

~

I once had to catch a train but had no ticket in hand. My dad dropped me to the station thirty minutes in advance; but I found that I was at the wrong station. I ran to the metro and then to the ticket counter at the other station and saw a huge queue. I ran to the unreserved queue, which too was very long. I was sweating and panting, but managed to persuade the folks at the head of the line to empathize with my situation and they let me in ahead of them. I got the unreserved ticket and ran to the platform, only to find that the train was thirty minutes behind schedule! I finally got a reservation and managed to sleep on the train that night. It would never have been possible had I said to myself, there is just no way I can make it to the right station on time and get the ticket and then catch the train, all in twenty-five minutes. Stay positive, focus on the small wins, do your best and more often than not, you will reach the finish line with a smile. Don't end up overanalysing the situation and remain stuck at the start line. To my way of thinking, it is important to keep executing, self-correcting and patting yourself as you go along, rather than spending a huge amount of time strategizing and planning for the perfect move, while crucial time is ticking by.

Now none of this is rocket science but I find that most of us, myself included, don't follow these simple principles most of the time. We then get caught in a downward spiral rather than catching the upward thrust.

~

Running is a simple and a reliable tool to start getting you to practise this. If you are just starting to run, the following comprises what a 5-kilometre run is.

A 400-meter run followed by a 200-metre walk, again a 400-metre run and 200-metre walk, followed by a 2-kilometre slow jog, and the 400/200-metre run/walk thrice over again. Now that sounds much less intimidating, doesn't it?

So start running and get your mind prepared for the big one! There are many major challenges to deal with in life. My goal here is to help you to help yourself; actually, with the propulsion and elation you feel after a run, it will feel like rocket science!

In fact, I would like you to say to yourself after you have read this: "I knew this all along, I did not need to read this chapter to be told this." And then, get on and act, don't overanalyse your situation.

Thinking big and doing the big one requires big physical and mental training in between. If you are planning your first marathon or half-marathon, I would definitely suggest that you follow a good training schedule, be disciplined and maintain a log to check how you did. The end goal is to become your own best coach now.

> "Don't train so hard for the marathon that you feel tired on the starting line. Many runners train too hard, and then end up with less than a full tank on race day."
>
> – Fernando Cabada, 2008 US Marathon Champion

Running long distance should ideally be based on a good training plan.

I find Hal Higdon's schedules for running different distances, simple, logical and well explained, and effective. Try the full marathon training plan shown in Table 9.1.

Try this with some discipline and you will see yourself getting ready for the big one.

Table 9.1

18-week Marathon Training Schedule (by Hal Higdon)

Training for your first Full Marathon							
Week	**Monday**	**Tues-day**	**Wednes-day**	**Thursday**	**Fri-day**	**Satur-day**	**Sunday**
1	Rest	4.8 km	4.8 km	4.8 km	Rest	9.5 km	Cross
2	Rest	4.8 km	4.8 km	4.8 km	Rest	11 km	Cross
3	Rest	4.8 km	6.5 km	4.8 km	Rest	8 km	Cross
4	Rest	4.8 km	6.5 km	4.8 km	Rest	14.5 km	Cross
5	Rest	4.8 km	8 km	4.8 km	Rest	16 km	Cross
6	Rest	4.8 km	8 km	4.8 km	Rest	11 km	Cross
7	Rest	4.8 km	9.5 km	4.8 km	Rest	19 km	Cross
8	Rest	4.8 km	9.5 km	4.8 km	Rest	21 km	Cross
9	Rest	4.8 km	11 km	6.5 km	Rest	16 km	Cross
10	Rest	4.8 km	11 km	6.5 km	Rest	24 km	Cross
11	Rest	6.5 km	8 km	6.5 km	Rest	25.5 km	Cross
12	Rest	6.5 km	13 km	8 km	Rest	19 km	Cross
13	Rest	6.5 km	14.5 km	8 km	Rest	29 km	Cross
14	Rest	8 km	9 km	8 km	Rest	23 km	Cross
15	Rest	8 km	16 km	8 km	Rest	32 km	Cross
16	Rest	8 km	21 k m	6.5 km	Rest	20 km	Cross
17	Rest	6.4 km	9.5 km	4.8 km	Rest	13 km	Cross
18	Rest	4.8 km	6.5 km	3.2 km	Rest	Rest	Race

Note:

Cross training is basically doing any aerobic activity other than running, be it swimming, cycling, tennis, badminton, or foot-ball.

Training too hard is like constantly focusing on retirement savings and stressing out about it, and actually succumbing to a heart attack in your prime, never getting to enjoy the life you had planned out. Another thing that long distance running teaches one is to stay focused and sensible about training. Taper off once in a while as required. And, most importantly, end with a big smile at the finish line.

Dream your dream.

Plan and train to get ready.

Break it up in smaller bits and execute.

Stay focused and committed.

Celebrate wins along the way and cheer yourself on.

Smell the roses along the way.

> Go for the big one — because it is your life to enjoy; that's why you are on this planet. Go live your dream.

~

10

~

The Panoramic View

"It is not the mountain we conquer,
but ourselves."

– Sir Edmund Hillary

Hillary enjoyed the view from atop Everest and soaked it in. That meant more to him than the achievement of being the first person to climb the world's highest peak. Sachin Tendulkar would give one amazing batting performance after another, and yet he always said that he was not chasing records . . . he was just going out there to play, enjoy the game and do his best. It just so happened that he kept creating history in every format and every field he played in.

This is what it's all about: going beyond performance and enjoying the view. These people epitomize achievement and have gone way beyond. That's the thing that struck me — running longer distances or faster or better is not about the records and the personal achievement, but more about going beyond achievement. It is more of a spiritual experience . . . it is just great to be there.

> "I had as many doubts as anyone else. Standing on the starting line, we're all cowards."
>
> – Alberto Salazar, three-time winner of the New York City Marathon

So if Alberto Salazar could feel nervous, we are all entitled to feel the same at the starting line of something big that we are about to undertake, any major project, or a run for that matter. And just as Alberto Salazar then went on to win the New York Marathon three times over, we too will see the glories of the "finish line," but we have to make it to the starting line first. The important thing is to feel confident at the start, to know that you have it in you and that your reserves will kick in when you need them. With a little humility you will listen to your body and everything around you, recalibrate if required, and stay focused on the learnings of training. And then fly past the finish line, enjoy the view and soak in the joy!

Do you get a kick from finally getting to the corner office or from enjoying the view from there? If you can't enjoy the view then you may have just wasted a lifetime, because there are so many things you have given up, lost so many friends, potentially rubbed so many people the wrong way, or made choices of work-life balance that left out much of life. It's no wonder that work-life balance is becoming an important mantra of working life — you don't want to end up burnt out, divorced or suffering from poor health.

The Runners High, Spirituality, and Tranquillity

> "For me, as for so many runners, there really are no finish lines. Runs end; running doesn't."
>
> – Dean Karnazes

The runner's high kicks in when your body starts to produce morphine endogenously in response to a run of 30 to 45 minutes, or longer. This has finally been documented in tests in German labs, so this is no longer in the realm of a crazy runner's mumbo jumbo. Also, given the explosion in distance running in the last decade more and more people, including several Fortune 500 CEOs and heads of state are experiencing that "high" and then going back for more. Often, when I am running or chatting with other runners, they say that after the first half-hour or so running is really easy and the kilometres tick by effortlessly. This is when they are in "the zone," where tranquillity sets in, the body is in a state of bliss, and if the natural surroundings are pleasant and the weather good, it doesn't get any better. The runners high does not come with walking, no matter how much you walk or how fast you go. So to my walker friends I say, "Push yourself a little more and experience the high."

For the Tendai Monks of Mount Hiei above Kyoto, Japan, long distance running is a powerful means to get to another state where nothing else matters. They seem to transcend this world and mentally propel themselves forward, onto a higher plane, as they achieve greater tranquillity and spiritual evolvement. James Davis writes in the *London Observer* about them, and I quote:

> The ultimate achievement is the completion of the 1,000-day challenge, which must surely be the most demanding physical and mental challenge in the world.
>
> Only 46 men have completed the 1,000-day challenge since 1885. It takes seven years to complete, as the monks must undergo other Buddhist training in meditation and calligraphy, and perform general duties within the temple.
>
> The first 300 days are basic training, during which the monks run 40 kilometres per day for 100 consecutive days. In the fourth and fifth years they run 40 kilometres each day for 200 consecutive days. That's more or less a full marathon every day for more than six months.
>
> The final two years of the 1000-day challenge are even more daunting. In the sixth year they run 60 kilometres each day for 100 consecutive days and in the seventh year they run 84 kilometres each day for 100 consecutive days. This is the equivalent of running two Olympic marathons back-to-back every day for 100 days.
>
> The running style dates back over a thousand years. "Eyes focused about 100 feet ahead while moving in a

steady rhythm, keeping the head level, the shoulders relaxed, the back straight, and the nose aligned with the navel."

What makes all these distances even more amazing is the manner and the conditions in which the monks run. These runs are usually begun at night and are over mountain paths that are uneven and poorly marked. During the winter months the low temperatures and snow are a great hindrance to the runners. These monks do not wear the latest in footwear and clothing, but run in straw sandals. They also run on a diet of vegetables, tofu and miso soup, which modern athletes and nutritionists would deem to be unsuitable for endurance events.

They have to carry books with directions and mantras to chant, food to offer along the way, candles for illumination, as well as a sheathed knife and a rope, known as the "cord of death." These remind the monk of his duty to take his life if he fails, by hanging or self-disembowelment.

During these long runs the monks must make stops at temples of worship that can number up to 260. This means that the 86 kilometres run can take up to 20 hours to complete leaving the monk with very little time for recovery or rest, but as an old saying goes: "Ten minutes' sleep for a marathon monk is worth five hours of

> ordinary rest." They also learn to rest sections of their body while running, such as their arms or shoulders.
>
> When the Japanese Emperor maintained his court in Kyoto, the monks were afforded a special thanksgiving service in the Imperial Palace after completing their 1,000-day term and the "marathon monks" were the only people who were allowed to wear footwear in the presence of the Emperor.

Then there are the ultimate beings — the Tarahumara (or Raramuri) Indians of Sierra Madre, Northern Mexico, a long unheard of and unseen tribe. Their basic dwellings were finally discovered at altitudes of between 6,000 to 8,000 feet. Their members are known to have run distances of 200 to 300 miles at one go without any problem. I can imagine meeting up with one at O'Hare Airport at Chicago and hear him say, "Too bad I missed the flight, got to run to Detroit now!"

The closest likeness I can find to the Tarahumaras are the Sherpas in Nepal and their feats of climbing Mt. Everest and other Himalayan peaks with physical ease. Both live at high elevations in remote parts of the world, lead simple lives and are, attitudinally, and perhaps otherwise too, closer to heaven than any other beings on our planet. No wonder they possess capabilities that seem superhuman to the rest of us. Many have tried to study the reclusive Tarahumara to understand how they manage to do what they do, wearing "shoes" made of tyre rubber, and living on a diet of simple corn and squash. We, on the other hand, cannot achieve a tenth of that on the best of diets and with the fanciest of apparel, shoes and gadgetry. We have a lot to learn from them.

In his fantastic book *Born to Run,* Chris McDougall describes how Coach Vigil, one of America's all-time greats, watched the Tarahumara run a 100-mile ultra marathon in Leadville, Colorado. Watching them scramble happily up the dirt hill, while the other runners looked determined and tired, he felt he had finally found "natural born runners." Over the past several years, he had collected a lot of data about runners across the world, but now he realized that it was not about how to run better, but more about how to live and live with zest. Now he knew where he was going to get some real answers. That is truly running and living.

~

Much has been written about the connections between running, spirituality and tranquillity over the last decade.

Sri Chinmoy, a spiritual teacher in the Sri Aurobindo Ashram in South India in the early 1960s, had also been a decathlon champion. He would encourage his students to combine meditation with running. In his book *The Outer Running and the Inner Running*, Sri Chinmoy writes:

> Our inner running definitely helps us in our outer running. Through prayer and meditation, we can develop intense will power, and this will power can help us do extremely well in our outer running. Meditation is

> stillness, calmness and quietness, while the running consciousness is all dynamism. Again, the runner's outer speed has a special kind of poise or stillness at its very heart. An airplane travels very fast, yet inside the plane we feel no movement at all. It is all tranquillity, all peace; and this inner tranquillity we can bring to our outer life. In fact, the outer life, the outer movement, can be successful only when it comes from the inner poise.

Warren A. Kay, a professor of theology at Merrimack College, Massachusetts, and author of the book *Running — The Sacred Art: Preparing to Practice,* writes that, "The act of running is a simple but solitary act that allows one to clear the mind and 'do a lot of thinking.' It gives the runner an excellent opportunity for spiritual development, regardless of membership in a particular religion or sect."

Interestingly, according to Chris McDougall, who researches evolution, the human species was born to run — not fast, but long. According to him a track runner at age 19 peaks by the age of about 27, then tapers off, and then comes back to his 19-year-old peak performance at the age of 65! So there is hope for all of us — start whenever you want to and don't use age as an excuse for inertia.

~

Running and Meditation

Here is a take from Urmimala Dutt, a friend and a healer, who focuses on going beyond the physical body, with running.

> "Let the body think of the spirit as streaming, pouring, rushing into it from all sides."
>
> – Plotinus

This is a very powerful visualization to hold in the mind while running. Your running experience will be completely meditative and transformational.

Truly, for people who have heard meditation is great for body, mind and soul but find it very difficult to actually meditate, running could provide the answer . . . and holding the above mental picture could have mind-blowing results where physical, emotional and mental benefits are concerned.

So, get, set, go! The rhythm of running regularizes your breathing and as it does so, it slows down your brainwaves to meditative levels. As your brain waves slow down, stress leaves the body and your personal power grows.

As your feet hit the ground, energy rises up your legs into the spine — opening up the "root chakra" at the base of your spine. Chakras are energy vortexes, or analysis centres in your body, deeper than the physical level. When the chakras are open, you are mentally and emotionally healthy and the physical body is immune to disease.

An open and well functioning root chakra grounds you in the world and takes care of your ability to handle basic needs — the *"roti, kapda aur makaan"* (food, clothing and shelter) issues of life.

As you run, the energy moves up the spine from the root to the "sacral chakra" — this is your emotional centre at the lower stomach area. An open sacral chakra corrects imbalances in your relationship with yourself and others and promotes creativity in your life.

Keep running and let the energy flow up your spine to the "solar plexus chakra" in your upper stomach area. This is your power centre. Energy moving through your power centre enables you to succeed in the material world. You effortlessly "do what you have to do."

Now feel the energy moving to your "heart chakra" in the centre of your chest. This centre governs your ability to give and receive unconditional love . . . releasing the need to judge yourself or others and allowing the energy of forgiveness to flow in.

As you continue to run, the energy rises up to the "throat chakra" — the centre of self expression and self responsibility. As this centre is energized, you feel empowered to speak out your truth and are able to take responsibility for whatever happens in your life. You begin to realize that your world is your mirror and essentially reflects back to you who you are, giving back to you what you give out.

The vision broadens and your perspective shifts higher as the energy rises to the "third eye chakra" between your eyebrows. When this energy centre is clear, your "pattern recognition" ability is heightened. You no longer miss the woods for the trees. You gain clarity of mind and the ability to "see" your way out of blocks or confusion.

The crowning glory of spiritual growth and realization come when the energy rises to the crown — opening you up to your full potential as a human being at harmony with oneself and the world . . . . Enjoy the runner's high!

So keep running — keep the energies humming. Keep healing your life. When you raise your energy's vibratory frequency with an activity like running, you will notice that you are attracting better things in your life.

This is because like energy attracts like energy. So when your energies are high, you attract high vibrations from the world, in terms of success, harmonious relationships, opportunities and joy.

~

"They can because they think they can." – Virgil

I have delighted in running marathons along the beaches of Rio where the party-going Cariocas (residents of Rio) thought we were crazy, as they showed off their bronzed tans and played beach ball in their bikinis. I've loved running in Paris along the Champs De Elysees with snow around and the first rays of dawn peeking through the clouds; winding through the canal streets of Stockholm and the old city lanes of Gamlastan. I have run in Shanghai along the Bund and along the Han river in Seoul; past Rashtrapati Bhawan in Delhi; the Emperor's Palace in Tokyo; up and down the tree-lined roads in Nairobi; on Table Mountain after the Two Oceans in Cape Town; in the picturesque and tough Great Ocean Road marathon in Australia with its koala bears; from the snowy and elevated base camp of Mount Everest, and more. Running has allowed me to truly enjoy what is around, and see sights like never before, taking in nature, the urban sprawl and the varied hues of humanity in my stride, as I ran in summer, winter, and the monsoons. These are experiences I would have missed, or perhaps not appreciated as much, had I been whizzing by in the air-conditioned comfort of a car. I didn't start running because I wanted to experience all this. I got into running by accident. But what a great accident it has been! I've enjoyed the panoramic views and that, to my mind, is ultimately what it's all about. To be able to enjoy life to the fullest, and appreciate the wonder that is nature and what is around us.

That's why I smile when people ask me how long I ran, or what my pace was, or what position I finished, and I just say, "I enjoyed every bit of the run."

So in the whirl of today's world, where careers, work-life balance, nuclear families, ever-rising expenses and widespread turmoil keep us all on a roller coaster, all in a bid to show that we are going great guns, getting richer, and supposedly feeling happier, running is one way to build a bit of tranquillity within, to look at ourselves from the inside and outside, engage in some introspection, and move forward. Remember Sri Chinmoy's aeroplane analogy . . . running enables us to get a high, and get "into the zone" and feel energized and positive. It enables us to break barriers and build self-confidence and optimism. Whenever we lose sight of the humility we need, either through injuries or through performance at some level, we are brought back down to earth. It enables us to not just become better runners, but live better and more complete lives . . . in fact, running pretty much enables us to live life to the fullest.

Think of running as a way of getting more from life. Running is not an end in itself. Make a start if you have not already, or push yourself into unchartered territory if you are already a runner. Get to enjoy the panoramic view that life has to offer.

Start running — and living.

~

11

~

Everest Base Camp Marathon

Learnings from a Fabulous Journey

Everest, here I come — gulp!

My 50th full marathon had to be a big one, so I chose to attempt the Everest Marathon, from Everest Base Camp (EBC) to Namche Bazar, on 29 May 2014. This was my way of celebrating the "50 Marathon" goal I had set for myself in 2002, at the time of my second marathon in Chicago.

The easy part was telling everybody and myself about it. The tough part was to try and raise some funds to pay for it, and to train so that I could finish with a smile.

A meniscus surgery (most likely from mountaineering in my teens and skiing in my forties, I must add hastily) in my left knee in August of 2013 had kept me off running for four months, but 2014 saw me as a pacer yet again for the party animals, and several first timers, at the Mumbai Marathon in end January. That was fun as usual, but for me it was my 49th and it also gave me the confidence that all was well and I could at least manage a slow marathon without any injury. I had run many marathons but the highest so far had been at an altitude of 11,300 feet. The highest climbing I had done had been up to 20,000 feet, but that was when I was in college. Now, at fifty-four, starting a marathon at 17,800 feet was another experience altogether. This would be one heck of an adventurous marathon — one of the most exciting in the world!

Thursday, 15th May / Delhi

There comes a time when you are close to achieving some goal — but then you realise that you are also pushing yourself to the limit. And you wonder what the heck you are doing! Well, this was one such moment for me as I started reviewing the list of things needed for the Everest Marathon — headlight with spare batteries in case you get lost or take longer than ten hours and it starts getting dark, a whistle, wound cleaning kit, compression bandage, a huge medical kit and a whole host of other things. Meanwhile, I also packed a harmonica, asked the organizers if they could arrange a guitar for the 12-day trek, because I felt it would help in relaxing while acclimatizing. I also eagerly carried the Nikon 610 full frame camera that I had ordered especially for this adventure.

As a mountaineering enthusiast in school and college, I had been fascinated by Everest and had always dreamt of making it to its base camp. Now I would be going there in a different avatar — as a marathon runner. I thought that would get me to appreciate the approach to the base of Everest as much as the mountain itself.

Saturday, 17th May / Kathmandu

Woke up at 4 a.m. and Kurt my roomie, who had come in from Hong Kong just a few hours earlier, was up and bright too. 4.57 a.m. was when we reached the hotel reception with all the bags and left in two groups of 22 each. The Twin Otter 14-seater taking us to Lukla made the air ride an experience, as it was the smallest plane I had ever been in. A half-hour later I realized that this was the only size that could make it to Lukla airport because it has a sharply inclined airstrip that is all of 400-metre long. It was quite an amazing landing even for Kurt who flies for Cathay.

Briefing, teaming up, baggage check and a few hours later we were off, past the Lukla airstrip, and on the track to Everest Base Camp. I wondered how many thousands of people walked on this route every year to climb Everest or one of the many peaks around, and several more to trek to Everest Base Camp — EBC.

An Irish Pub, German Bakery and more . . . Lukla was buzzing with activity, a far cry from what used to be grazing pasture land before Tenzing and Hillary's climb in 1953.

As we trekked along the Dudh Kosi Valley (Kosi meaning river and Dudh — milk — because of all the rapids and the crushed rock/sand, which made for a milky river), the mule track we walked on was wide but rough enough to fuel the excitement of what was to come ahead.

We kept a slow, easy pace and chatted as we went along. The fun part about an easy paced acclimatization with many stops is that you get time to chat with everyone, individually and collectively, and laugh, joke and bond.

Ulfat, a climber from Israel was the first Palestinian woman to attempt this marathon.

Susan Weeks, a gritty and tough 72-year-old, 150-time ultra marathoner from Los Angeles was all set for the challenge.

Steve from Cape Town had completed many triathlons and a few marathons.

Diane and Rex from Adelaide were here because Diane had gotten into ultra running after starting off with a 10-kilometre run just five years earlier.

Shaun from Canada and Shogo from Tokyo were rooming together and had run several exciting marathons themselves.

I was in crazy company! When I mentioned this to my wife on the phone post Lukla, her plea was simple — "Please don't get inspired by anyone there!"

We passed several villages along the way and the loveliest one, in the Solo Khumbu District, was just called Ghat 6. The houses looked really inviting, much like Switzerland perhaps a hundred years ago. I felt I could settle down here for a few months every year. At our destination we had a great dinner of soup, rice, dal, boiled veggies and papad, and then off to sleep like a baby. Twenty rooms in the lodge with one toilet and one washbasin between them; very luxurious, as I would find out later.

Sunday, 18th May

The sun came up pretty early and our alarms set to a precision wake-up time of 6:30 a.m. for a 7 a.m. breakfast were not of much use as the bright sunlight woke us up at 5 a.m.

Oats porridge, two boiled eggs, toast and tea later, we were off towards Namche Bazar.

The trek comprised of steady ups and downs, with a few suspension bridges *en route* to the gateway of Sagarmatha National Park. I think the Indian National Park managers could learn a few things about park management from here — general cleanliness, friendly staff, no touts, and no hard selling of photographs, gear and snacks. No wonder many foreigners feel so much more comfortable visiting Nepal.

About 7 kilometres and a net 200 metre height gain later, the trek started getting more rugged. The Dudh Kosi gorge narrowed and we started the steep climb up as we left the river roaring down below. We then came to a set of two suspension bridges high above the Dudh Kosi and crossed the river on the upper one, which was a good 300 metres above the river and over a hundred metres long. Going over it was an experience in itself. Thereafter, the ascent continued; switchbacks, less chatter, a bit of singing to cheer things up, a 200-metre altitude climb and then we came around to Namche Bazar. A sigh of relief went up as we caught sight of the first homes and hotels.

The nice and comfortable Sona Lodge was our home for the next two nights. Everyone was tired but feeling great. Susan came in an hour after us but she was looking good as well. We had been really lucky with the weather so far with no rain, but unfortunately the forecast for the week ahead seemed much more bleak.

Monday, 19th May

Susan and Harry were both not feeling good in the morning. The rest of us went out for a leisurely walk and got our first views of Ama Dablam, Lhotse — and Everest! The light was too bright to photograph the snow peaks but we tried our luck in any case.

Tuesday, 20th May

The first blow: Susan on oxygen and evacuated by helicopter to Kathmandu. Harry also looked like he would have to go down. Meanwhile, I was still debating whether or not to have diamox as a preventive for high altitude sickness. I hadn't slept too well the night before with a bit of heavy breathing and had tossed and turned weighing the side effects of diamox *versus* being evacuated by a helicopter later on. All but three of us were on diamox by now. I decided to start on the preventive dose.

The start of the trek was a straight, stiff climb from the lodge to the top of Namche Bazar. This here was the finish line of the marathon, and we all went and checked out where a few of us would finish!

And then started a really steep ascent, from 3,400 metres to 3,800 metres, an attitude gain of 400 metres compressed into just one kilometre, breathtakingly beautiful, up past the tree line, on to the dirt airstrip of Shangboche, and then on to the Everest View Hotel. The gradual pace helped since this was no race yet — all of us had to make sure we acclimatized well and did not mess-up due to any heroics. I was carrying tons of water, apart from a warm jacket, windcheater, snacks, etc. in my backpack, along with the heavy camera bag. Since all this was good for acclimatization, I chugged along. Being quite cloudy we only got snatches and quick peeps of some peaks, but the route was gorgeous as we descended to the twin villages of Khumjum and Kande, past rhododendron and other flora. Dianne from Australia, Ulfat from Israel, Samir from Nepal and I did the walk down together. At one point the clouds started clearing a bit and we got some stunning views of Ama Dablam. The light, however, was too harsh for any even half decent photographs of the mountain.

Khumjum is yet another orderly and clean Sherpa village with the fields neatly lined with stone boundaries and all the stone homes having green corrugated tin roofs.

We reached our lovely inn run by an Italian owner and his Sherpa wife, and then took a walk around to a monastery, which housed an ostensibly authentic Yeti scalp and then to the Kande Village Hospital. I was impressed by the simplicity of the people, the non-commercialisation, lack of peddling wares and begging in this high tourist traffic location.

Unlike the previous night, I slept really well after a lovely pasta and cheese dinner and set my alarm for 4:30 a.m. in the hope of catching, some pictures of Ama Dablam by sunrise.

Wednesday, 21st May

It was foggy and misty at 4:30 a.m., but I could make out the shadowy outline of Ama Dablam through my window. So I dashed off to the dining area with a blanket and camera and lay there facing the window, opening my eyes every few minutes to check if the fog had cleared. I got to see some interesting light displays around the peak with a rainbow halo and changing lights. Around 5 a.m. I walked out to the school and around the Paradise Inn Lodge to get different angles of Thamserku and Ama Dablam peaks.

8 a.m. saw us depart for Thyangboche and rejoin the marathon route. This stretch was going to be a tough section of the marathon with a 100-metre ascent to Thyangboche

Monastery, a 600-metre switchback drop down to the Dudh Kosi river, then across a suspension bridge, followed by a 500-metre climb up towards Khumjum and, finally, a 5-kilometre or so rugged trail run back to Namche. We were doing this route in reverse and it was a killer — the switchbacks, the terrain, the weight on the back, and the continuous, unending climbs gave us a taste of what was in store on race day. Most of us added on a few hours to our earlier estimated finish times. However, we were also rewarded with spectacular views around Ama Dablam, a rhododendron forest, some phenomenal views of the Dudh Kosi Valley and more; all well worth it!

When we reached Thyangboche Monastery, one of the holiest Buddhist sites in the region, we were delighted to be able to go in for a while and sit in silence while the fifteen monks there chanted, amidst the sounds from a huge drum, some horns and clanging bells. Time really stood still and I wondered what, if anything, may have changed here over the last two-hundred years.

A delightful, huge bakery just below the monastery was where we decided to go for coffee and snacks. I downed a cappuccino and shared some apple pie — both of which were delicious. There were great views of Everest, Lhotse and Nuptse, and many a snap was clicked in different poses.

A scenic descent through the flowering rhododendron forest then took us to Debuche village and the really posh Rivendell Lodge. There were absolutely phenomenal views of Everest and its neighbouring peaks from the dining room, garden, and even from our room! I spent five hours just clicking pictures from different angles with varied settings, hoping that at least a few would come out right.

The high point of the evening was hot towels at dinner, so all of us felt fresh as daisies as we had a good meal followed by our nightly briefing of the next day's plan.

Thursday, 22nd May

One week to go for race day. We started on the lovely trail up to Dingboche that ran all along the river till our lunch stop. We then crossed the river and trekked up another valley. The trail started through a rhododendron forest with white and pink flowers in bloom, with a descent of around 100 metres or more, a stretch we would have to ascend during the marathon. Then followed many descents to the various streams to cross bridges and then climbing back up again onto the trail. We had beautiful views of Everest, Lhotse, Nuptse and Ama Dablam until a few clouds covered them. The climb, altitude, backpack and camera bag were tiring, especially with the continuous switchbacks after every river crossing. As we walked, we were all adding more hours to our re-estimated marathon finish times. We finally arrived at Dingboche 5 hrs and 11 kilometres later with approximately 600 metres of net ascent, overall perhaps 1,000 metres of gross ascent. Our lodge was just above the tree line, with only juniper and other scrub around.

Friday, 23rd May

This was a rest day for acclimatization at Dingboche and as part of that we went for a 6-kilometre trek up and down the Vivre loop that was part of the route we would be running. While it was only a hundred metres higher than where we were, it, however, involved an overall height gain of more than 250 metres owing to the numerous uphill and downhill stretches. Meanwhile, I had lost track of the overall gross ascent and I wasn't sure if my cell phone with the runkeeper app would hold out for the duration of my marathon run. The 3-kilometre trek up from where we expected to get cell phone coverage was humbling but gorgeous. There were lots of group photographs and merriment as we went up, and then a few of us ran down the track to acclimatize.

Saturday, 24th May

We set off on our way to Lobuche with the usual 7 a.m. breakfast and 8 a.m. departure. Ulfat was down with a stomach bug and she vomited ten minutes out on the course. This was a bad time to get the bug but she still had a few days to recover, Shogo was steadily recovering from his tummy bug. I was getting a sore throat so my running towel doubled up as a muffler at night. I had unfortunately left my warm throat guard behind in Namche in one of those numerous weight and volume cut backs of gear that we were advised about. We trekked over juniper-lined rocky trails and saw Pheriche village down below us with the Pheriche Kola river flowing in its wide valley.

We kept glancing back to see what the trail would look like when we ran down it. We had to make sure that we did not descend back to Pheriche but kept onwards to the stupas above Dingboche, and then onto the Vivre loop . . . lots of things to keep in mind while running down on the 29th!

We reached the terminal moraine of the Khumbu Glacier, and the main memorial to many who died on Everest and the neighbouring peaks in the region — a solemn and humbling moment.

This section was more runnable, but at an altitude of more than 4,500 metres, I was sure that we would be gasping for breath while running even here. A few more uphill climbs later we reached the village of Lobuche, just as the weather packed up and the clouds came in. There were many helicopter landings on the helipad just outside our lodge. I wondered how the Italian pilot of the chopper managed to land on a tiny 10-foot by 10-foot "helipad" in such poor visibility and bad weather, and then lift off within thirty seconds of dropping his cargo and picking up his passenger. We were hoping he would be dropping a cargo of meat for our dinner, but no such luck. The guitar that was to have made it from Namche a few days ago to Dingboche was now back again at Namche. So I told Pasang Sherpa, our leader, to let it be and not to bother now. In any case, I would be too breathless to sing and play the guitar, plus my throat was now sore.

Sunday, 25th May

We started our trek up to Gorak Shep, situated at an altitude of 5,150 metres. This walk was spectacular. The valley opened up and offered many a panoramic view. The Khumbu Glacier was below us and we could see several glacial pools, seracs and the icefall coming down from Nuptse, just as the swirling clouds moved up the valley to keep Everest shrouded from view. Going up and down on the moraine was tough and we realized that we would have to be extra careful, especially when nearing the downhill sections here on the rocky terrain, apart from managing to stay on the right track.

Pumori, the perfect peak, was now visible and it really had us mesmerized. So as we huffed and puffed upwards, we felt it was more than worth the effort.

A few more uphill sections later we were delighted to reach Gorak Shep. I was really looking forward to the next day's trip up to Kala Patthar at 5,550 metres both for better acclimatization, as well as for the gorgeous panoramic view of the Everest range that the top provides. The plan was for a 4 a.m. start for most folks and I decided to keep Harry and a few others company and start at 3 a.m. I now had a headache and had lost my voice, so to protect my throat I had stopped talking, I am sure much to the relief of my mates. A few medicines later I fell asleep at 8 p.m. after dinner. It had been snowing mildly from 4 p.m. but nothing much to worry about.

Monday, 26th May

Got up at 3:40 a.m. as the 3 a.m. start had been scrapped. Got ready with all the layers — three on the legs and four on the upper body, with socks on top of my ski socks, and stepped out with my trekking pack, water, concentrated sports drink (magic potion) into a white-out — there was snow everywhere and the visibility was down to 10 feet. The 4 a.m. trip was called off and we were told to come back for breakfast at 8.30 a.m. Even then the conditions had not improved enough, with around 3 to 4 inches of snow and poor visibility of around 100 metres, which could drop to 5 metres at any time. It was decided that two groups would set out — the first would trek to Everest Base Camp and back and the second to Kala Patthar. I bravely opted for the latter. We set out at 10 a.m. and slowly started the snowy and rocky climb. It was amazing how quickly a lot of us were getting out of breath. Michael turned back after 50 feet, then Di and Rex too decided to turn back after another 100 metres, and finally Craig and I also decided to return — there was no view and it would take a few hours to get back down even in clear visibility. I was not willing to risk going higher and then slipping on the way down, with no view as an upside.

As we trekked higher the toilets in the lodges became more and more basic. In Namche we had running water and flushing toilets, while now there was no running water and water had to be chucked into the flush to make it work! Meanwhile, the temperature dropped steadily as we gained altitude from

13,000 feet in Namche to 16,500 feet in Gorak Shep. Each bit we ascended provided a learning on how important the basics of life were, and how much we had to be grateful for.

Meanwhile, the snow continued unabated and Kala Patthar, black as stone when we had trekked in to Gorak Shep yesterday, was now white with deep snow. I felt a mild fever and so took some paracetamol and went to sleep waiting for the big day to get to Everest Base Camp.

Tuesday, 27th May

The snow was coming down thick and fast as we made our way through breakfast, downing the porridge and eggs and looking out of the window, waiting to get out. My throat was much better and the fever had subsided, but now a headache and a stomach-flu had both kicked in. This marathon is a pharma company's delight. I was hoping I would get these two issues out of the way by the next day, to be able to focus on the run down.

So while the snow fell incessantly we trudged up and forward gradually. My childhood dream of getting to Everest Base Camp (EBC) was on its way to being fulfilled. I was not focused at all on the run . . . it was all about the trek to EBC from Gorak Shep. Another ridge, then a descent to cross a gushing river, and up again to get closer and closer to EBC.

A great cheer went up from the leaders of the group as the tents at EBC came into view. Our amazing porters had already carried our big bags and made it to Base Camp to set up the tents, the toilet tents and mess tents — while the snow kept up its onslaught.

Hot tea and soup later, we had another round of diamox to act as a preventive for altitude sickness. The only downside to diamox was that you had to drink tons of water and, thus, pee every few hours, including at night. Kurt and I got into our tent and set up our thermarest air mattresses on top of the foam mattresses that had been laid out. We attempted to snooze but struggled with heavy breathing and wondered how we would last the night, and then yet another. I thought about all the nights of our college expeditions and school treks, staying at high altitudes and realised that I was now tending towards being claustrophobic and would need to give up my sleeping bags and tent living after all these years, when finally I had the great equipment I'd yearned for earlier.

The dinner was terrific. It was a luxury to get hot food on our plates at Everest Base Camp. Everest did not want to be seen and the tragedy of the Sherpa lives lost on the mountain was fresh in everyone's minds and all we could see were clouds and tents and a few bits of the Khumbu Icefall whenever visibility improved.

We trudged back to our tents and got ready for our first night at EBC while the snow kept coming down. We were lucky there was no wind else it would have been crazy. Every five minutes the tracks to the 70 tents were obliterated and we slipped and went waist deep in parts when we went off the "track." It took fifteen minutes to get inside our tent as Kurt and I dusted the snow off our jackets and our shoes, and paused to catch our breath. Our tent was on a bit of a slope and that was going to make sleep all the more challenging, particularly as I was still coughing like crazy and was worried that Kurt would be the next group casualty. In all we got up fifteen times to kick and shake the top and sides of the tent to clear the snow off and reduce condensation; twice the tents were cleared from outside by the phenomenal staff of the organizer.

We were three days from a really tough marathon and under normal conditions we would be resting, carbo-loading and staying off our feet.

Were we actually going to be able to *run* here?

Wednesday, 28th May

The decision had been taken to move back to Gorak Shep. There was simply too much snow for us to start the run from EBC — it had never been so bad in the thirteen years of this event. I was happy, since the night had been rough on me and I would rather start after a night's sleep in a lodge at Gorak Shep as opposed to a tent at EBC — wet, cold, a bit claustrophobic and then having to pack everything before the run.

So began the move back to Gorak Shep. But for the life of me I could not find my sunglasses; they were not in the mess tent, nor our tent or my running pack. I have to thank Pasang our leader and seven-time Everester for gallantly lending me his sunglasses to use on the way down to prevent snow blindness, even though it was overcast and snowing. We began our slow and somewhat dicey descent down a freshly made slippery track. The glacial lakes were beautiful, made somewhat more ethereal by the low visibility, the clouds and the falling snow. That 5-kilometre trip took a long time and it was almost as if Everest did not want to reveal its face and yet wanted us to be close by for as long as possible. We had stayed a night at EBC — a privilege reserved only for mountaineering expeditions, and now for the marathoners. That was a treat in itself.

Since many of the porters had already been sent back down, we were now carrying heavier loads than when we were coming up, and the conditions made it tough going, not the best thing to do in lieu of the usual total rest day before a gruelling marathon.

Two Brazilians who were just behind us seemed dehydrated and we gave them water and some munchies. Later the next morning we were horrified to learn that both were down with snow blindness since they had not worn sunglasses the day earlier. They were airlifted down to Kathmandu, as was another couple also down with snow blindness, and another participant who had to opt out after an hour of the race for the same reason; a grim reminder of what all could go wrong.

Reaching the start line with no injury and in a fit condition was a feat in itself, as many of us were depleted with headaches, stomach flu, fever, poor acclimatization, and much more. Over the last few days I had been hit by laryngitis, stomach flu (which luckily lasted only a day), fever and a headache — all of which, under normal circumstances, would have made me pull out of the run. But here running was also the quickest way down the mountain! So I quickly scratched out any Plan B from my imagination, popped paracetamol for the fever, lozenges for the throat and cough, got into my race gear, added a few layers, and after a great dinner went off to sleep.

There were so many learnings for me as I slept dreaming of the start line the next day, and drawing comparisons to life:

- Health, truly, is wealth.
- Simplicity is what we need to bring back into our lives in a variety of ways.
- The unexpected is to be expected.
- You can only prepare so much, and then you need to think on your feet and keep progressing towards your goal.
- When you take on something really big, seeking help, advice and support from others makes a huge difference.

~

12

~

On Top of the World

D Day — 29th May, the 2014 Everest Marathon.

Flag-off time — 8 hours 8 minutes and 48 seconds in the morning (the height of Everest is 8,848 metres).

Flag off time was approaching. The previous evening was actually spent trying to figure out what clothes to carry — would it be warm or cold? Wet? Windy?

I decided to wear my leggings, long sleeve compression T with the race T on top, along with my windcheater — I was not going to carry any warm gear as I was targeting to finish in around 9 to 9.5 hours, which would be around 5.30 p.m. No spare shoes either, just my heavy-duty trail shoes. I carried a few extra socks, borrowed Pasang's sunglasses again, took my earmuffs, a headband and light gloves. A roll of TP for emergencies, two bottles of water, one bottle with a sports drink, chocolates, raisins, cashews and seeds to munch, additional Gatorade powder and salt to make some more sports drink at the half way point — and I was about done. I hadn't slept much at night though the paracetamol had brought the mild fever under control and my coughing was a bit better. I rolled out of bed, went to the Gorak Shep toilet for one last time and said to myself — "Never again!"

The crazy 60-kilometre ultra had been flagged off at 6 a.m. and now we were being led to the start line with our names being called for a final attendance — definitely required in this sort of race.

So here we were — calf- and knee-deep in snow at an altitude of 17,000 feet and ready to start our run. We were already battered and bruised in the most part — but that was only physically — mentally we were all raring to go.

The countdown began and in a few moments the 50 Nepalese were off — they ran as if this was some flat road race at sea level. Then followed the 100 foreign participants — a few running but most of us walking, trying to catch our breath because the first uphill section appeared almost immediately. The sky was clear and I had set a 90-minute goal for those 5 kilometres to Lobuche. I had no walking sticks, which would have been a boon on the run down. But then I was soon on a level part of the track made slippery and icy by the 50 to 60 people ahead, and started a slow jog with small steps. I felt great and continued till, whoooosh! I was down on my back having slipped. The snow was soft and so was the landing. I got up and started walking again. There were smiles on our

Author posing before the start line at the Everest Base Camp

faces as we stopped frequently to take photographs and videos of this phenomenal experience. Then, slam! Down I went again with my right hand once more breaking my fall. This time my arm went down shoulder deep into the snow — but this was nothing to worry about — other than telling myself that I had better walk, rather than jog, on this snowy and icy section. So I continued down as did the 50 others behind me and we tried to quicken our pace wherever possible.

I reached Lobuche in around 1 hour 20 minutes and was delighted at being on track with my target time. The snow continued beyond Lobuche to Thula and the Memorial with all the prayer flags at the end of the Khumbu Glacier. Everything looked so different from when we had seen it just five days ago — no snow *versus* everything enveloped in white. We paused for a minute's silence in this serene spot where the memorials were set up for so many from across the world, united in doing what they loved to do — climb.

The flat section, where all of us had thought we would speed up, was now full of mushy melting snow, water puddles and juniper, and we crisscrossed around in our now squelching shoes. Started running again and on a few occasions had to get my right arm out for balance. That's when I felt a shooting pain come down from the shoulder and I realized that some damage had been done to my right shoulder and wrist. But I did not know how bad it was and decided that it was safer to give it a rest by walking as briskly as I could.

I was frustrated that I had to walk on this flat section, which was still snowy and mushy, but kept up a decent pace nevertheless. Craig was about a kilometre behind me. Then came the stupa above Dingboche and as I looked over the ridge on the left I saw the Vivre loop of around 10 kilometres — scenic but incredibly tough with steady uphill going before the descent. On the right was the route towards Pangboche, and onwards to Namche.

The Everest Marathon a few kilometre into the race

I went quickly down the track to Upper Dingboche and towards Vivre. There I met Rex and he and I downed some hot soup and a few sips of water at the aid tent. I left my backpack there and continued up the loop. We met Steve and Chris as they were finishing the loop, looking somewhat drained but going very strong. Saw many other participants coming down from the top of the loop and encouraged those who looked broken, going up. "This is impossible! I can't do it!" gasped some as I passed them. I said that they were almost at the half-way mark of the marathon and told them to think of their friends and family who would be thinking of them right now, and to carry on.

Saw Samir at the U-turn point of the Vivre loop, which was an uphill without end. The peaks around were a visual treat and a reward for all of us as we finally made it to the half-way point and began the 5-kilometre descent. As I came down, I met Lara, Harry, Bee and Ulfat and several others. The sun was by now covered by clouds that had come up the valley and the wind had upped its speed a little, though luckily it was not too cold. Now I had begun wondering if I should have gotten my fleece jacket along too. But no point crying over spilt milk, I was just glad it was not too cold.

Back at the junction the noodle soup I had been dreaming about for the previous two kilometres was over. So I picked up my backpack and started the journey down from Dingboche to Pangboche somewhat disappointed. I was alone and met trekkers and porters and villagers as they made their way up the mountain track. A steady drizzle began. The rain was exactly what I had been dreading — but then again — luckily, there wasn't a strong wind. My windcheater kept the rain at bay and I started dreaming about ordering a noodle soup at the next village. I was so hungry! I reached a small restaurant in Pangboche and ordered a soup. Meanwhile, I tried to find a big plastic bag for my daypack as well as for myself or even an umbrella, but without any luck. The noodle soup was great for ₹ 300 and after another selfie and an Fb post, I carried on down. I had lost around half-an-hour with this stop but felt it was well worth it as I felt rejuvenated and the rain did not matter any longer.

Thyangboche was the next stop and the steep switchback descent to the river began. I had to be careful about not slipping on the wet gravel sections of the track. Soon I came across Gunther and Monique from Germany and I shared some raisins with them as we continued pretty much together. We crossed the collapsed bridge and then started the climb to Thyangboche Monastery — up though the rhododendron forest with white and pink flowers, past Rivendell Lodge in Debuche where we had stayed a night, and then the climb continued, as we got closer to Thyangboche. That's when I got a fright — red pee. This was a sign of severe dehydration, although it could have been something else too — so I glugged down my water, gave more of the salty snacks to Gunther and Monique and tried to keep my mind off it. An hour later we were on the other side of Thyangboche making the 500-metre descent to the river *via* steep switchbacks over 3 kilometres. Even after I had downed two more bottles of water, the pee was still the same deep red. I called up Pasang and told him what was happening. He also felt that it was most likely acute dehydration and that I should drink more water and meet the doctor at the next checkpoint. So I kept drinking water but when I finally reached the checkpoint the doctor was not there. I filled up more water and drank again and then met Sahara and Bindra, two of our Sherpa guides, who were walking back to Namche, and they joined me. I gave them my dark Toblerone chocolates since I could not have them with my dehydration — and now all my snacks were finished.

~

The steep and never-ending climb towards the Khumjung turn had begun. Every five minutes I needed to stop for a few seconds to regain my breath; and perhaps take a photograph every now and then. I asked Sahara how much longer to the top, to which he said thirty minutes. The sound of the gushing river waters seemed more and more distant as the last of the 1,500-feet climb was done and we reached seemingly level ground.

It was here, to my delight, that I met with Smiley Norbu, a 60-kilometre ultra runner who was coming in tenth. We started chatting and he decided to walk with me to the finish. We chatted about what he was doing in college in Pokhara, his French godmother who had funded his education, and his dreams of doing adventure camp training in India. The music from his cell phone kept us going as the shadows became longer and the light started fading. It was around 7 p.m. now. I told him that I desperately wanted to finish while there was still light as I did not have a headlamp and had only a small torch with me. Chatting with him kept me off worrying about my red pee and dehydration, though surprisingly I was not feeling weak at all.

As we passed the final aid station, I filled my bottle for the last time. I picked up the Indian flag kept there for me and Norbu took a Nepali flag and a French flag for his godmother. It was dark by now and out came my small torch flashing away brightly ten feet ahead of us on the rocky track. We trudged along and after what seemed eternity, we finally saw the finish line and ran towards it, arm in arm, with the flags held high in our hands. We had finished this run together and I had completed my 50th marathon!

We hugged each other, got our photographs taken and then I collected my tracksuit and certificate. We continued down to our lodge to a boisterous greeting from those of our group already there — I was able to only whisper my delight at having joined them since my voice was again gone. I remembered the moment at Pangboche in particular, when I had been tempted to consider the option of sleeping the night there and continuing the next morning, which was permissible under the race rules. I was glad I had pushed myself to continue. This had been decidedly the most gruelling and punishing run of my life — about ten marathons rolled into one experience!

I told Colin, an anaesthetist from Melbourne, about my red pee. His opinion was that apart from dehydration, the busting of some capillaries with the downhill running and the associated pounding could have caused it. He felt that if I did not have any other symptoms of dehydration, the latter could potentially be the issue.

I could not have beer given my throat condition so I settled for some Khukhri rum. It felt great! So with my throat feeling better I downed some delicious mushroom soup. There was mutton curry awaiting us and I gobbled a few helpings of that as well.

After another round of Khukhri rum I decided to book a shower for ₹ 300, and also decided to have a shave, without a mirror though since there was none there. I returned to the gang a cleaner and a less smelly version, with the 10-day stubble removed in parts from my face! And, most importantly, the pee was colourless — the Khukhri rum had done it! I told Colin and Pasang about the magical medicinal properties of Khukhri rum! It was amazing — we were strangers when we had come together a fortnight ago, and now we were discussing bowel movements and more!! Everest had brought us really close together!

Namche Bazar was a most comfortable home and we had a great evening as Pasang got out a birthday cake for Kurt's 40th — he had cracked it in an amazing time of 6 hours 42 minutes. A Pole who had come in first had finished in around 4 hours 20 minutes — amazing timing, especially after suffering a few broken fingers on a fall. One Nepali ultra runner was down with a fracture and was being airlifted to Kathmandu. We were champions all, delighted at having been humbled, but not humiliated, by Everest.

~

The next two days were spent trekking back to Lukla — full of fun and chatter, although I could not speak yet. We reached Lukla on May 31st and spent the night at Buddha Lodge just overlooking the airport. But before we departed for Kathmandu we had an important event — for our party of participants, along with the porters and our support staff.

We pooled our tips together, along with the gear that we were not going to take back and divided everything into piles each with a number, and the staff had a lucky dip. They were delighted and each one did a little jig and went around shaking our hands. They had been great, selflessly waiting on us attentively and shaking off the snow from our tents at base camp at 2 a.m. and 3 a.m. in the morning, and more importantly — always smiling. We may never see them again but I know we will always remember them and learn from them about some aspects of life — working with passion!

Sunday, 1st June

We got up at 4.45 a.m. and were ready by 5. 30 a.m. and down at the airport. Group A had got onto the first flight of Tara Air and we were on the second plane. Waiting in the departure lounge for our craft to come in, we saw a Sita Air flight from Kathmandu land and then, all of a sudden, twenty people ran towards the runway as sirens began wailing. The Sita plane apparently had a jammed right wheel brake and veered to the right on this short 400-metre airstrip and almost went off the side of the runway. The pilot then jammed on full power to get the plane to keep going up the 15% inclined runway and safely offloaded the passengers. It was frightening.

Our Tara Air flight landed fifteen minutes later and without any undue excitement we boarded and were at Kathmandu airport 30 minutes later.

That night the party continued with steaks for dinner and some shopping along with Kurt.

Monday, 2nd June

I went to the Himex office and met with a supplier who took me to a printing house where I got portraits printed onto

Friends forever: Smiley Norbu and the author at the finish line at Namche Bazar

mugs and a group photo on a slate for each member of our group.

We were bruised, sunburnt to the core with our lower lips double their normal size, licking our wounds, and nursing torn muscles and more. But we could not be happier. We were all on top of the world!

And then we had a wild farewell party at Shanker Hotel, hosted by the organizers — wine, beer, dancing, chatting and celebration, that's what it was all about, along with much sobbing that we were leaving each other the next day to go back to our various homes across the world.

Two weeks earlier we'd been strangers, now we were mates.

Part 2

~

Going Beyond

Now that you have seen how people across the world, across your country and in your neighbourhood have started going beyond what they thought was possible for themselves, I hope you have started to experience some of the positives in your journey. I would like to briefly touch upon the role running can play in building and cementing relationships in your personal and social network, and then go beyond into getting people together as a community of runners to do things for the community. And ultimately look at how companies can experience a significant impact in their bottom line *via* running — which then makes this activity or lifestyle, sustainable.

13

~

Sweat Equity into Relationships

Run Together, Bond Together

"The best friends that I have today are the people in my running group. I started running just a year ago."

This is what I used to initially be surprised to hear, but I have now heard and seen this, thousands of times. I started experiencing it myself too once I finally found human company on my runs. The stray dogs and cows were finally *passe*!

Shshank started running with us in Gurgaon and steadily got better and better. He started running some of our tougher runs in Shimla and longer runs in Gurgaon, and then the ultras. His young family with his sons, all of six and four, started taking part in some of our runs, first as proud spectators and then as runners, and Shshank's wife, Romilla, would be an enthusiastic volunteer — cheering, handing out certificates and, in the earlier years, looking after her younger son. Now, a few years later, she has run with us a few times and is training seriously; all four of them would then be running together. Bonding, holidaying, running, travelling, laughing, playing, getting medals together and waving certificates at the same event, gets the children to feel like grown ups and the parents feeling like kids. After her Shimla 6k, Romilla feels like a champ and Shshank after his umpteenth really tough Shimla Ultra Half Marathon swells with pride readying for their family photograph at the finish line. The run is over and the bonds are flourishing.

Mike and Anne from Malaysia always reach the finish line hand in hand. From the first Gurgaon Marathon in 2009 and then in Shimla, then in Corbett, and Rishikesh, and Gurgaon in 2014 and . . . . The smiles only get bigger.

Narayan and Divya go one step further by invariably running together as they did through our Himalayan Half Marathon in the paradise that is Sangla Valley and through various editions of runs in Shimla, Corbett, Gurgaon and Noida and finally their first full marathon in Gurgaon on December 14th, 2014.

During my 50th marathon I met a wonderful couple from South Australia, Rex and Di Bichard at Everest Base Camp. Rex is a great guy, quiet, a diver, has an abalone export business and got dragged into the run by Di after two not-so-enjoyable earlier running experiences while Di is the forever-laughing and joking person, who had been pushed by her sister, into a 10k run a few years earlier. She had recently run a 100k! The fifteen days of trials, travails and togetherness, both alone and with other crazy folk, only brought them closer as they trekked, ran, and partied together.

I would recommend the Everest Marathon as a perfect honeymoon because it would get the couple to get to know each other threadbare and, after whatever venting that would happen, they would be much the wiser and better bonded at the end of the experience. So watch out marriage counsellors! Running is the new thing.

~

Friends, couples, siblings, parents and kids, entire families and any other permutation that I may have left out, get together for a run and a getaway at some of the runs we organize on beaches, in forests, in the mountains, or in the cities. They sometimes push each other, cheer each other, test themselves individually, and re-discover their fire within. And then retire to have a guilt-free carb load of colas, or beer, or tons of food!

The motivation comes from that one crackpot family member who is addicted to running, who then gets others to first come as spectators, or to drive the car, and then they too take the foolish decision of participating in their first ever 5k run. After the medal, the certificate and the ritual photograph at the finish line, they 'unfortunately' get hooked and seek to get more people to sweat, and so it continues.

And while you run together with your spouse, your kid, your mother or your cousin, given all the endorphins and positivity, the phenomenal thing is that others get to see the best side of you, and you the best side of others. So all gets forgotten and forgiven as the sweat on the brow and the endorphins within, get us to bond ever better.

If you are the first runner in the family, then you need to do the job of selling running to your family members, because then everyone is happy. Else, you will be an absentee dad, mom, or spouse, which can also cause angst with your wake-up alarms ringing early morning, before the owls go off to sleep.

Sometimes when you run, it is the best uncluttered positive time you spend together — no phones, no email, no scrapping, no grocery shopping list, and no bills-to-be-paid list, everyone positive, and so on; most of the time.

Try it!

Tomorrow!

~

You can start changing what you do, step by step, from tomorrow. But surprisingly, what you do, unbeknownst to you, will have a much wider impact as friends, neighbours and colleagues may notice what you are doing and perhaps get inspired to do something similar. You may even become a bit of a running evangelist and perhaps bring a couple of friends out for a run with you in the mornings. The important thing is that running is not an end in itself, but a powerful means to an end — the end being unleashing our potential, both individually and collectively.

Running can be a very personal and individual pursuit. Several people like to run on their own for a variety of reasons — privacy, safety, not wanting to chat with strangers, time schedules, convenience of a run starting from your front door, listening to music and perhaps a thousand other good reasons. I was a solitary runner for the first nine years of my running life. Then occasionally I started running with a few people, and what a difference it has made for me . . . chatting, joking, laughing or just silently appreciating one another's company. At the frequent runs that we now organize in different cities across India, I see more people smiling and greeting one another, running together and chatting. Across the varied running groups in diverse cities and towns I have found people making powerful statements such as, "Some of the best friends I have made after school and college have been my running buddies."

It starts perhaps with a smile being exchanged at a run, then some light banter at the next run, and suddenly you have one more acquaintance. Runs together during week days further strengthen the bonds, and then the families get acquainted. A few picnics and runs later, the friendship is cemented. These include some gatherings at which there is no gender segregation, but a coming together of runners from varied backgrounds. Here most people don't care what car you drive, or where you live, or what your nationality or religion are. What matters is that you are a runner — some are faster, others are slower, some have just started and others have been running for ages. Runners on business trips from different cities or even countries link up with other runners and become friends for the run, or take up where they left off when they meet at another run, and then sometimes end up friends for life. That is the glue that binds, as acquaintances and newfound friends cheer for one another and hug each other at the finish line. A new community is formed.

> "Meet a guy in a business suit, and he could be a useful business acquaintance. Meet him sweating in shorts and a T-shirt on a run with you, and he is a friend, perhaps for life."

When people run together they exude positive energy, and long distance chats nearly always focus on something helpful or supportive. Invariably, the conversation turns to a charity that can be supported, or how to give back to the local community, or tree planting sessions or perhaps creating something more sustainable.

~

14

~

Transforming Your Community

"Ask not what your country will do for you . . .
but what together we can do for the
freedom of man."

– US President J F Kennedy, in his inaugural speech in 1961

In 2009, a week before a run I had organized in Gurgaon, I had sent out an email to our runners to bring any old clothes and shoes to donate to the kids of migrant labourers who lived in a shanty town along one of our running routes. The response was overwhelming; we had a few carloads of stuff sorted and laid out at the finish area. We didn't want to just donate it, but get the kids to "earn it" and feel proud. During our run we called all the kids and any adults of the settlement who were there (we had also told them about this the day earlier), and asked them to run with us to the finish. There all the kids got a pair of footwear and some clothes.

Proud runners with the clothes they have won at the finish line

Watching their joy in finishing the run and getting some goodies brought tears to many an eye. Stuff that we were going to throw away was of such value to others! It put things in perspective for many of us; some of us focused on the need to recycle things and "give back to the community" in some way; others thought of linking up with non-governmental organizations where they could help out. Somewhere, this had started making an impact on everyone's lives.

> "Running brings about a unique positive energy to a group, and gets them to do what they perhaps may not otherwise think of doing."
>
> – Running and Living

At another one of our runs we planted saplings, and watered them. We engaged parents and children, CEOs and villagers alike.

At another run, we had runners pick up trash along the route. At the finish line we handed out a finisher pack in return. The feeling of satisfaction was palpable on several faces.

"Tiny drops of water make the mighty ocean."

At a run in Corbett Park we had runners bring in their children's books. We ended up with many suitcases full of them, and set up a library in the village school in the fringe area of the forest.

And the list goes on.

Governments, brands, local businesses and local communities — open your eyes to what running can do for all of us together!

~

Now if there are 10,000 runs across 10 weekends a year in several neighbourhoods across the globe, each doing what is near and dear to that area, A LOT CAN BE DONE. Sometimes these actions and the time spent has a greater impact on participants, the media and observers, and kilometre by kilometre, these acts start to make our world a much nicer place to live in. City, district and village administrations could experiment with such runs, which are non-competitive and inclusive. They will be amazed at how people become infected with the idea of running and break barriers and get a little more "good" happening.

> "Running a marathon starts with the first step."
>
> – Running and Living

The first New York City Marathon in 1970 had 127 participants, with the runners doing several loops around Central Park. The run now goes through all the five boroughs, gets about 40,000 registered runners, and over two-and-a-half million spectators line the streets. It generates over US $250 million in business for communities in and around the city. This comprises transportation companies, hotels, restaurants, tourism, shopping malls, marathon support industries — water, T-shirts, jackets, medals, volunteers, event management, audio visual, and more. It is quite a spectacle! The entire city gets energized. In Boston, the marathon is held on a Monday and businesses in the area shut down for this annual event.

This simple activity called running can bring about a lot of change. It's almost a miracle!

> "When people get together in running shorts and T-shirts, the sweat of running makes 'barriers' fade, and gets people smiling, to make acquaintances and, later, friends for life."
>
> – Running and Living

15

~

Enterprise Transformation

"If you focus on best practices you are playing catch up. Create 'next practices' for others to follow."

– C. K. Prahalad

Unknowingly, my wife's uncle C K Prahalad had a profound impact on my fledgling entrepreneurial venture. I was fortunate to have met him several times and during the last few meetings I had outlined what I was doing. I wanted to focus on the next practice and go to realms where people would say, "But I think this is crazy!" That's when I could seriously rethink, introspect, and hope that I was on to something.

I believe that running is the next golf. It is the platform on which the next billion deals will be made, friendships forged and the outdoors explored — across beaches, forests, cities and mountains.

Running builds communication within and across teams, and reducing the amount of "bcc" (or "blind copy") emails in companies.

Having worked in Unilever, Nestlé, a small Indian firm, Motorola and now my own venture, in different capacities of sales, marketing and business management in national, regional and global roles, I believe there are two keys to business success; teams consumed by their focus on the consumer, and product innovation. Enterprises however often ignore the following two major points:

1. Getting each individual to fire at his or her potential.

2. Building a high performance team to deliver the offering.

Too often, and this is no magical observation, a team of three means at least two paths, if not three, that are being followed, even after a decision on the way forward has been taken.

The benefits of people running as a path to good health leads to reduced absenteeism and stress, and its attendant knock-down effect on team performance and customer delivery and delight.

Beyond these tangible benefits of health are other benefits, such as building perseverance, self-confidence and optimism for each individual. The impact of this is much more powerful, though it's much harder to measure.

A corporate team celebrates at the end of one of our runs

Leadership traits of looking beyond, having the ability to look at a big, hairy, audacious goal, taking risks, changing tack as required, and developing supreme optimism and self-confidence become especially important for those in decision-making positions. These aforementioned qualities also need to come with a decent dosage of humility and improved communication skills; traits that many of us seem to lose as we climb up the ladder in our organization, be it governmental, corporate or a not-for-profit one.

You are running a company, but is your company running?

That's what I ask senior management at the start of a brief immersion exercise before the workshop we do with the wider management team. I list out a bunch of hidden costs and metrics — attendance, medical costs/insurance, employee dissatisfaction levels, commitment, and therefore underutilized fixed administration costs — in the organization that can be used to measure tangible and intangible costs associated with personnel that often go unobserved. When it typically gets quantified at a whopping 10 to 20 per cent of personnel costs, management teams tend to forget about their backache and comfortable posture and sit upright, some in shock. The enormity of the hidden issue is compelling.

At the workshops I provide to organizations, I continue to find that participants, from the president to the trainee, become kids again, hierarchies disappear for a while, and people begin to talk while running, ending in a huge amount of chatter once the run is over. The energy shift becomes quite palpable. That's what I find regardless of size, culture and type of business, as I discuss hard and soft metrics for monitoring progress with human relations (HR) and business heads to make sure this becomes an organic activity and builds continuously. My work within Motorola in Global Market Research on brand management, and then with the Global Human Resources team on developing and living the internal brand promise for the corporation, has been of great value to me in building these workshops and working with senior management on hard and soft metrics of measurement.

The administrator of an engineering college where I organized a run in 2007 was delighted after my talk to the students and the succeeding run. He said, "I have started cycling with the students as they run the 5k and 10k and all of a sudden I find them opening up much more to me and talking about things they never used to otherwise. It has resulted in many constructive suggestions coming from them."

> Running impacts an organization both internally and externally and adds a new and permanent dimension to the bottom line. This is a defining next practice for business in the 21st century.

The biggest kicker for a company, I believe, comes when they use running as a potent marketing platform and then as a 360-degree ecosystem engagement platform.

~

Epilogue

~

"Running is the next golf, only a hundred times bigger."

As I finish this book, it's been eight years since I left Motorola to start my venture to build running into a marketing platform in India. It has taken a lot of commitment and a lot of focus to keep going and not dilute the offering. For example, along the way a few friends asked me to consider the spectrum of wellness. On introspection, I realized I knew very little about that vast field and my competency and credibility lay in the route I had chosen to individual wellness, which was running, and building it into a marketing platform. Slowly but surely, my 25 years of marketing experience was being put through its toughest test.

~

I started focusing on running as a 360-degree platform for organizations — employee engagement, teamwork, productivity and bottom line enhancement, innovative customer connect to engage HR, finance and marketing stakeholders across potential client organizations.

I also started communicating the 360-degree marketing benefits that we could provide in our customisable runs — of getting the company's ecosystem engaged; employees as volunteers, customers and relationship managers, suppliers, brand ambassadors and other stakeholders participating in the runs in varied capacities.

In 2012, Apple was declared the world's most valuable brand ever. This is one brand that has shown razor sharp focus, with each offering enhancing its brand value rather than becoming a messy conglomerate of sub-brands and products, some of which have little relevance or linkage to the mother brand, as seen in the case of many other companies that use the corporate brand as their market face. From the iPod to the iPhone to the Macbook Air to the iPad, it's been quite a journey, but a focused one, with the results for all to see — business results, loyalty among consumers, and brand strength. Apple thinks out of the box, thinks and executes in a 360-degree approach, and delivers a revolutionary experience. Even their retail stores have been game changers for many in the retail business.

This is what my fledgling start up marketing venture — Running And Living Infotainment, is about. Here we are focused on consumer engagement with the client brand in a unique and fun manner, which is measurable and hugely leverage-able in a 360-degree manner.

So when people ask me, "Why running? Isn't it limiting or too narrow? Why not look at overall wellness and a bouquet of activities?" I tell them that this is one activity that spans each and every aspect of your lifestyle and your outlook to life. It gets you focused on your diet, sleep, posture, flexibility and strength and improves each one of them. And you will get into each of these aspects because running is addictive and you will always want to run longer, or run faster. And to do that, there is no other way but to take a holistic view of each aspect of your lifestyle.

Running provides a base for building self-confidence and optimism.

Running works wonders with organizations and with the broader community too.

Though I started quite by accident, it got me running and living. Maybe you can try it too, and see yourself changing.

Start running and living.

Just take the first step, and see how you feel after two weeks.

In 2014 at our Running And Living Half Marathon at the Formula One Race Track we had our sponsor vehicles on the track and also available for test drives by a select few participants, making it much talked about on social media, and great for photo ops.

Employees, customers, products and services, dealers, suppliers, corporate clients, media, corporate social responsibility activities, and more, for one organization — all find a common leverage platform in a very positive and fun filled atmosphere. That's what our big dream at Running And Living is about — getting 200 million people inspired into running, enabling organizations and brands to engage in a fun way to achieve their objectives, and making running a sustainable platform for both personal transformation and organizational change.

~

Starting off in 2007, the first year was spent in running related material being disseminated *via* print, TV, radio and digital media to millions of households — why run, how to start, what you should wear, where you can run, etc.

The second year was spent doing free runs in Gurgaon once a month and learning from the participants — what happens in summer, during the rains, in winter, during the festive season, exam time and more, and what are the things other than running that get people satisfied about a morning well spent — sapling plantation, book donation and clothes donations to underprivileged, running with kids with special needs, clean-up runs, getting people focused on water, the environment, wild life, saving beaches . . . .

And then we started with runs in other cities and runs where people had to register in advance and pay for, and running groups across the country which were self help local groups, and a social network and outreach *via* Facebook and Twitter, and improved communication *via* a variety of channels. We have now done over 200 runs across 11 states of India. Opportunities of expansion, collaboration, partnership and help have come in from several quarters, some totally unexpected. I had torn up my business plans several times over in the first year and, now, though I have a blue print of where we want to go, how soon and which opportunity comes up first does not happen in as structured a fashion as I was used to in my salaried corporate career.

First, people thought I was crazy when I quit my job and started planning my marketing business focused around running.

Then people could see I was passionate about running but saw I had no experience in organizing a run.

Then people saw we had done multiple runs, but looked for more options.

Now we offer a portfolio of up to 30 options annually, in a manner not done by anyone else in the world. We have made a start.

The tougher the run, the bigger the smile and the more cherished the medal at the finish line. This is at Rishikesh – our toughest half marathon

If you are not a runner and have reached this page, I would love you to start running and use the earlier chapters to get you over some physical and mental humps.

If you are a runner, I would love to have you integrate what you are experiencing *via* running, into your work and personal life, to internalise this lifestyle and it's value to you, even more.

My dream is to do 500 runs all across India and I am not sure exactly how it will happen as we franchise, inspire others to start runs on similar lines in different places, and look at ways to explode the numbers of people running regularly, but I know that it will happen.

With your help, wherever you are in the world, we will make this happen, together.

~

Notes

~